Richard Marshall is a Private Client Solicitor with over 10 years' experience in advising clients about Wills, Succession and Inheritance Tax Planning, Trusts and Estate Administration. Having taken a keen interest in Blockchain technology and Cryptocurrency since 2016, Richard now advices clients on the key considerations about leaving Crypto Assets on death, the difficulties in balancing Private Key security during lifetime with accessibility on death, and the tax treatment of Crypto Assets on death, as well as advising Personal Representatives about the practical and technical issues associated with administering Crypto Assets and the risks involved for the estate.

Richard has delivered training nationally on the topic of administering Crypto Assets as part of an estate administration and is due to speak at an international conference on the difficulties of dealing with NFTs on death.

A Practical Guide to Estate Administration and Crypto Assets

A Practical Guide to Estate Administration and Crypto Assets

Richard Marshall, Solicitor (TEP)

Law Brief Publishing

Published 2022 by Law Brief Publishing, an imprint of Law Brief Publishing Ltd
30 The Parks
Minehead
Somerset
TA24 8BT

www.lawbriefpublishing.com

Paperback: 978-1-914608-62-9

PREFACE

Technology is changing at an alarmingly fast rate, and with it, opportunities to commoditise and profit from these changes are arising at equal speed.

This is no more so apparent than in Crypto Assets, particularly Cryptocurrencies and NFTs. Whilst market volatility has seen dramatic falls in value around the time of writing, those early adopters and investors are still holding considerable gains and will leave valuable assets in their estate if they were to die.

This new and evolving asset class of Crypto Assets presents unique challenges to the current legal framework and to those providing advice to Executors and Administrators of estates (referred to throughout as Probate Practitioners).

It is essential for all those involved in advising in the administration of estates to have a basic understanding of the nuances of Crypto Assets and the practical considerations and pitfalls when dealing with this new asset class as part of an estate administration.

In preparing this Practical Guide to Administering Estates with Crypto Assets I would like to thank my long-suffering wife for her patience and support, and my parents for instilling in me a love of learning and a confidence to be curious.

It is confirmed that at the time of writing on 14 October 2022 the stated law is believed to be correct and up to date.

Richard Marshall
October 2022

CONTENTS

PART ONE

BACK TO BASICS

CHAPTER ONE

DIGITAL V CRYPTO

The current legal reality

Let's begin with a stark reality: ownership of Digital and Crypto Assets is a legal enigma. At the time of writing, the UK Law Commission have launched a consultation on Digital and Crypto Assets, recognising that they do not fit within the current legal definitions of property.

By their nature, Crypto Assets cannot be real property, and under current legal constructions can only therefore be some form of personal property. Personal property itself has two categories – something you can physically hold (a chose in possession) or something that can only be obtained through legal action (a chose in action).

On the face of it, Crypto Assets do not fall within either legal definition of personal property. This issue was looked at in the context of Cryptocurrency in an unreported case of *Robertson V Persons Unknown* from 2019 regarding cryptocurrency fraud, and again in the case of *AA v Persons Unknown [2019] EWHC 3556* which was a cryptocurrency extortion case. Following this it was confirmed in the cryptocurrency fraud case of *Fetch.ai Ltd and another v Persons Unknown Category A and others [2021] EWHC 2254 (Comm)* that, in the court's opinion, Crypto Assets are a chose in action.

From these cases, it is clear that the current legal framework has an uneasy relationship with Crypto Assets.

For now, however, these cases give some reassurance to anyone acting as a Personal Representative of an estate which holds Crypto Assets.

Given the court's interpretation, these cases can be looked to as authority for Crypto Assets falling within the Personal Representatives duties under S.9(a) of the Administration of Estate Act 1925 (as amended) to *"collect and get in the real and personal estate of the deceased and administer it according to law"*.

Given that these recent judgements place Crypto Assets within the duties of Personal Representatives to correctly administer a deceased person's estate, it is therefore fundamentally important to, at least have an awareness of, and at best to fully understand, how these assets work.

In light of the difficulties in the relationship between the current legal framework and Crypto Assets, it is therefore helpful to perhaps start with something with which many will be more familiar.

The 'traditional' digital estate

Most practitioners are now acquainted with the concept of a digital estate. This can include things such as social media accounts, online bank accounts; auction accounts, betting accounts, email accounts, music libraries stored on Apps, and video streaming accounts, as well as the electronic devices on which these assets are accessed and stored.

Whilst some of these assets have a clear monetary value, some have a more sentimental value, and a paradigm shift in estate administration has arisen with regards to the latter. The days of leaving your CD collection and family photos to a relative or close friend are largely gone. Now, we see what can at times be described as a bun fight over access to social media accounts to retrieve, preserve and share treasured memories in the form of photographs, posts and content. We also see wilful violation of user agreements in the form of passwords being shared, and devices accessed, after the death of the asset holder as most of these agreements are made up of non-assignable licences.

For all the familiarity and interaction with digital assets, as mentioned, we are still very much in an unregulated space, with the law applicable to assets in the physical world struggling to translate and be effective for their digital counterparts.

One big positive, however, is that with most digital assets, there is still a third party with 'control' over the accounts held by the deceased. If there are any difficulties in locating or accessing these accounts, there is still hope that the organisation hosting the site will be able to assist. There is (in theory) a human being behind the screen who can be reached and reasoned with in order to resolve the difficulties of locating and accessing digital assets and many site are also now making provisions for circumstances where an account holder dies.

Where once there was a concern about online and paperless bank accounts removing the paper trail of breadcrumbs that Probate Practitioners so often rely upon, there is now the realisation that the majority of online banks in this Fintech space can be contacted and a search undertaken to ascertain whether the deceased held any such accounts with the relevant online bank.

For many users, however, this Internet Service Provider centric approach to online content has been a blessing and a curse. For anyone creating and uploading content online, autonomy over that content is largely lost once it is uploaded to a website. Fundamentally, the third party 'hosting' the website has ultimate control over the accounts which are created and the data which is provided. It has led to an online eco-system focused on monetarising data which in turn is able to drive marketing and promotional advertising to then enable creators to financially benefit from what they upload.

For any practitioner acting in the administration of the estate of an influencer or content creator, understanding this eco-system is key to being able to effectively administer the estate and ensure the assets, and income streams, of the estate are correctly administered after death.

Estates with Crypto Assets – the future is here

Control and transparency are therefore the order of the day for a new look internet – often dubbed as 'Web 3' – and for many, at the heart of this, are Crypto Assets.

This new wave of internet has seen a move away from third parties hosting content, to communities validating within themselves what they do, which has been underpinned by Blockchain technology.

The focus of Crypto Assets is therefore a Decentralized model of self-regulation, allowing ultimate control and the promotion of transparency. There is also a large focus on security, with cryptographic methods of generating addresses (public keys) and passwords (private keys) for accessing and transferring Crypto Assets (as well as verifying the transactions – for example through mining crypto currencies), adding to the immutability of the technology behind the assets.

There are, of course, a number of paradoxes within this model; where the Decentralised nature of the network allows for transparency around the transactions it records, it also allows anonymity of the end users; where the cryptography creates security the self-regulation leaves the end user vulnerable to being locked out of accounts indefinitely (or until quantum computing can break the cryptography); and where the communities of Decentralised networks are still largely centred around sites hosted in the traditional way, it leaves them open to more traditional cyber security hacks and scams.

Why is any of this relevant? Well, this is the context in which Probate Practitioners are being faced with a relatively new asset class that must be administered on the death of the holder. Whilst this is not a study of the particularities of the technology or the mechanics of the ecosystems within which they operate, to fail to understand the basics of this is like being ignorant of how the stock market works in relation to the nuances of stocks and shares, not just with regards to share price fluctuations, but how income is generated and whether holdings are ex-dividend, entitled to script rights and so on. It is also fundamental to understand how these assets can be held, just like with stocks and shares which can be certificated, held as nominee by a discretionary manager and such.

It is also important to appreciate Crypto Assets as a different class of assets as opposed to what we would now describe as traditional Digital Assets. At the heart of this difference is the technology, and it is the technological footprint of Crypto Assets which also creates a new set of breadcrumbs for Probate Practitioners to follow when trying to first identify the Crypto Assets of the estate before moving on to access, secure and distribute them on behalf of the beneficiaries.

CHAPTER TWO

BLOCKCHAIN TECHNOLOGY

Blockchain technology comprises, in essence, the building blocks of the Decentralised Network within which Crypto Assets operate.

The Genesis Block

Every Blockchain starts with the very first transaction recorded in a block of data – this is known as the Genesis Block. A cryptographic code is created, followed by a code which represents the details of the transaction in question (such as the transfer of some cryptocurrency from one user to another) and this is then verified by other users in the network (referred to as Nodes), in line with the rules of the network (known as the Blockchain Protocol), before a final cryptographic code is created to confirm the transaction has been verified.

The final cryptographic code verifying the transaction is then used as the initial code of the next block, thus creating a chain of transactions represented by each block, which is transparent in the details it holds about each transaction and infallible in relation to the authenticity of one block to the next.

The information held within one block cannot be amended or tampered with by anyone without corrupting the chain. This is the reason why Blockchain technology is seen by many to be immutable, whilst also creating transparency because the decentralised ledger of transactions made between peers within a network is distributed for every user to see.

Transactional confirmation by Nodes

The transparency and immutability of the Blockchain also brings control, as it is the network of peers which verifies the content which is created and the transactions which occur between the peers within the community. This is done through what is known as 'Nodes' and is the biggest shift from what we currently have with the internet in its current form, as information is stored in a fixed location usually a server, and it is the control over the server which takes away control from the content creators. Similarly, it is the control banking systems have over personal funds and currency fluctuations which attracts people to cryptocurrency as a Decentralised monetary system.

For the Probate Practitioner the underlying technology behind Crypto Assets may well seem irrelevant, until of course it is. In understanding the way in which transactions are recorded and held in the Blockchain, it is then possible to find new breadcrumbs when collating a picture of the assets and liabilities of the estate. This could, for example, highlight; assets purchased by the deceased during their lifetime (which may not be apparent from the information held by the deceased on death); transfers of Crypto Currencies to other wallets (or accounts) owned by the deceased which were previously unknown; lifetime gifts made by the deceased in the form of Crypto Assets; and, from a risk perspective, it can help to identify any possible fraudulent activity on the account after death which can then be tracked and (hopefully) recovered.

Ownership on the Blockchain

So if Crypto Assets are in essence digital representations held within a distributed ledger on a Blockchain, what does the deceased actually own?

This is only answered with another question – how was the Crypto Asset purchased? For cryptocurrencies, there is a distinction between purchases on a custodian and non-custodian basis (the former giving you a right to claim your cryptocurrency and the latter giving you direct control of it). For NFTs and some tokens, as a starting point it is often a Smart Contract which governs the agreement transferring ownership of the NFT from one owner to another. However, depending on the platform through which it is purchased or the organisation through which it is issued, the rights associated with the NFT or token could still be governed by a third party (such as a traditional server based website or the members of a Decentralised Autonomous Organisations ("DAO").

An understanding of how Blockchain technology works, therefore, is only one part of the puzzle when it comes to understanding the Crypto Assets owned by the deceased.

CHAPTER THREE

WALLETS, DEVICES AND PASSKEYS

If Blockchains show us the transactions which have occurred and been verified within a network, how then are these transactions carried out?

Types of Wallet

A Crypto Wallet is required to deal with Crypto Assets. This in many ways is the gateway to the Blockchain. Each wallet has a pair of keys – one public and one private.

The public key is for want of a better description your Crypto address. It is the information which you would provide to another user so that they could locate you and, for example, transfer Cryptocurrency to you.

The private key is then the equivalent of a password. It allows you to sign off on any transaction from your wallet as a way of ensuring the user has authority to complete the transaction and deal with the Crypto Assets.

There are two categories of wallet – a hot wallet and a cold wallet.

A hot wallet is always connected to the internet. Due to this they are very easy to use and are convenient. This can be on a desktop or mobile device where the wallet is connected to the internet whenever the device is connected. This gives the convenience of using the wallet almost seamlessly with the devise, however, the wallet itself is only as secure as the device and due to its ongoing connectivity to the internet it is susceptible to malware, viruses and keyloggers (a virus which records keystrokes to record passwords and private keys). If the device itself is also compromised or lost then so is the wallet.

A hot wallet can also be hosted on a website. This is often a crypto exchange and highlights another difference between wallets, which are referred to as custodian and non-custodian wallets.

A custodian wallet is usually held by a third party like a crypto exchange which will retain a user's private key to sign off on the transactions the user initiates. Whilst this takes the pressure of ensuring the correct nature of a transaction from the asset holder, it gives up a large element of control. Some crypto exchanges have also confirmed that the crypto they hold as custodians would be used to settle outstanding creditors if the exchange was to become insolvent. Whilst this is no different to the relationship people have with their bank account (whereby the monies held by the bank can be used to settle outstanding creditors if the bank became insolvent), those investing in the UK crypto exchanges do not have the benefit of the £85,000 Financial Services Compensation Scheme which in essence guarantees cash held by a consumer with an authorised firm (usually a banking group).

By comparison, non-custodian wallets are those which are retained by the owner of the Crypto Assets. By their nature they therefore rely on the asset holder to retain all relevant access information about the wallet, as there is no third party to turn to should you find yourself locked out of your wallet.

The distinction between custodian and non-custodian wallets is often epitomised by the saying "not your keys not your coins" which highlights the way in which custodian wallets ultimately give up control of the wallets – and in turn access to the Crypto Assets – to a third party (usually a crypto exchange).

A cold wallet then, is a wallet which is held offline – that is to say not connected to the internet. The most common types of cold wallets are hardware wallets and paper wallets.

A hardware wallet often looks like a USB thumbdrive and can be connected to a computer or mobile device. It is the hardware wallet itself which stores the private key and this information never leaves the device. It is only the details of the transaction which are filtered through the computer or mobile device which makes this type of wallet very secure. Some people new to crypto assets may be put off by the technical nature of hardware wallets and, unlike some of the cold wallets, they are not free.

A paper wallet is the opposed to a hardware wallet in terms of technology. It is actually printed onto paper and will have the public and private key printed in it, with a QR code which will then link it to the wallet online through a device. The nature of the paper wallet does not lend itself to convenience and if the paper is lost or destroyed it will be near impossible to then access the wallet.

Public and Private Keys

As mentioned, the private key for a wallet will allow users (or custodians as the case may be) to in effect sign off transactions on the blockchain. In practical terms, it is a long list of numbers and letters in a sequence which is cryptographically generated. Some wallets also generate a Seed Phrase (sometimes referred to as a recovery phrase). This Seed Phrase is usually 12 or 24 randomly generated words which allow a wallet to be reconstituted if it is lost. In doing this, it gives ultimate control of the wallet to whomever holds the Seed Phrase.

For the Probate Practitioner, understanding where Crypto Assets are held and how they can be accessed is fundamental. Using a more traditional comparison, it is like understanding whether a deceased's investment in stocks and shares is held in certificated form, or by a stockbroker as nominee, or with a bank in an ISA, a fund manager in an OEIC or by a financial institution in a bond.

Just like our traditional comparison where you need to know which paperwork you will be looking for on death so that you can record the all-important account numbers and establish which organisations you have to contact in order to deal with the stocks and shares, so with Crypto Assets you need to be mindful of which devices may be relevant, which bits of paper with random letters, words and phrases may be important and which third parties – if any – you may need to deal with in order to identify and access the deceased's Crypto Assets.

Devices

It is also important to be aware that a desktop (or more importantly the tower unit), laptop, tablet, mobile phone or external hard drive could all hold wallets. There may then be devices you have never even seen before, which by their nature may seem unremarkable and irrelevant, but are in fact hardware wallets holding untold riches in Crypto Asset form.

The deceased may also have handwritten notes or printed pages of long sequences of numbers and letters, and what may appear to be lists of unrelated words or incomprehensible phrases within their personal papers. Such information could prove to be invaluable in accessing the wallets if it holds the private key or Seed Phrases or is even a hint towards either of these (as this could be the basis for a targeted attack on the wallet to hack it as a last chance of access). Such information could also be stored on any of the devices mentioned above, as screen shots/grabs, encrypted text files and such.

It is also important to appreciate that the devices through which Wallets are accessed can also be cause for concern. For example, there have been instances where Wallets have been accessed through devices which have cloud-based storage, and the default settings have saved passwords (and in the case of Wallets Private Keys) which have been entered through the device onto the cloud. The cloud account has then been hacked and, the Private Keys stored therein accessed. This has then enabled the hackers to gain access to the Wallet and defraud it of all crypto assets therein. Whilst having details of the device on which Wallets are stored and the Private Keys for accessing the same will be a huge help for Probate Practitioners who are advising Executors and Administrators, it is arguably as equally important to ensure that those Wallets and the crypto assets therein are then secured and protected as soon as possible.

If dealing with an estate where the deceased has not made it clear on what device their wallet is accessed, together with directions as to where private keys or Seed Phrases are held or stored, then it leaves those dealing with the estate in a very difficult position in trying to review all devices for some or all of this information. Without an understanding of how the wallets can be stored and accessed, it makes this task almost impossible and could put Executors/Administrators in the very precarious position of causing great loss to the estate through not being able to identify, access or recover Crypto Assets.

PART TWO

CRYPTO ASSETS

CHAPTER FOUR

CRYPTO CURRENCIES AND TOKENS

Having considered the technology at play and how it is used to store and access Crypto Assets, it is then important to consider the different types of assets which may form part of the deceased's estate.

Crypto Coins V Crypto Tokens

One of the most well-known Crypto Assets is Cryptocurrency (sometimes referred to as "Crypto Coins"). In essence, this is any digital currency which uses cryptography to secure a transaction on a decentralised ledger. They are usually the original currency of a Blockchain (often referred to as the "Native Cryptocurrency") and purchased through an exchange which incurs a transaction fee. When using Cryptocurrencies in a transaction, there is then a transaction fee (referred to on some Blockchains as a "gas fee"). For most transactions this fee is linked to verifying the transaction (referred to as "mining") and is written into the rules of the Blockchain (referred to as "Blockchain Protocols"). Cryptocurrencies are commonly used to buy things – as a medium of exchange – to trade or to hold in the hope that they increase in value

Crypto Tokens, however, are usually issued by organisations or projects that are built on existing Blockchains. Crypto Tokens have more functions as they can be used to access specific features within an organisation or project, to participate in decentralised financial products (often referred to as "DeFi"), for governance purposes within organisations such as voting rights, to represent assets held in the physical world and even for playing games.

From a technical perspective, Cryptocurrencies are governed by the Blockchain itself, whilst Crypto Tokens are largely governed by the smart contracts which underpin them.

The distinction is obviously an important one for Probate Practitioners, as the nature of the Cryptocurrency and/or Crypto Token will determine what the deceased owned, the rights associated with it and, arguably most importantly, its overall value. It will also impact on where the assets can be used, as some platforms will not support Crypto Tokens.

Whether it is a Crypto Coin or a Crypto Token, most of these are what is known as mined. Mining Cryptocurrencies is the method by which transactions on the Blockchain are verified and this is done by people competing to solve a cryptographic puzzle in order to verify a transaction. This process is known as Proof of Work.

However, those mining Cryptocurrencies do not do it for the love of problem solving or the greater good of the Blockchain. They do it because the person who successfully mines the transaction is then rewarded with payment in Cryptocurrency.

Although much mining is now done by large organisations with warehouses full of computers, some individuals will mine on their computer at home. It is more difficult and arguably not always profitable to do, but an individual can mine cryptocurrencies at home. Often, however, individuals will sign up to a mining pool so that there is strength in numbers when it comes to the pool being allocated blocks to verify (known as hashing). The individual will still mine but as part of the collective pool.

Alternatively, individuals can sign up to cloud mining where, in essence, you rent the miners and in return for an upfront rental fee you will receive a share of the cryptocurrency issued to the miner once the block has been hashed.

Whilst there are clear benefits to mining cryptocurrencies, anyone doing this at home will have invested money in the necessary hardware to actually mine and will be incurring heightened electricity costs to power the hardware. Any Probate Practitioner faced with a room full of computers mining cryptocurrencies therefore needs to be aware of the pros and cons of doing this, particularly at the base monetary level in order to establish whether it is profitable to maintain the mining activities. Similarly for cloud mining, this is based on a contractual arrangement at its core and it will therefore be necessary to review any such agreement to see what, if anything, the estate is contractually bound to undertake.

DeFi

The currency of, and on, the Blockchain has also led to a new world of financial products which are based in the decentralised arena and are usually peer to peer. Known as Decentralized Finance – or DeFi for short – it allows, amongst other things, people to lend out their crypto in return for interest and rewards, borrow against the value of their crypto, trade and even buy derivatives.

DeFi organisations also issue Crypto Tokens which can give to the holder; governance powers over the organisation, entitlements to rewards and, it is hoped, in time an increase in value on crypto exchanges.

DeFi products usually operate through software known as DApps (Decentralised Applications) which are generally accessed through a Wallet. Whilst many DApps enable the activities mentioned above, such as lending and borrowing, there are also other use cases such as monetarised social media and gaming DApps.

DeFi also enables Stacking, which in essence allows someone to use their Crypto as a way of verifying transactions on the Blockchain in return for income. Whilst transaction verification is traditionally done through mining, Stacking is a way for transactions to be verified by people who have Stacked their Crypto, which is known as Proof of Stake. This is popular as it moves away from the energy intensive process of mining and is hoped will make transactions on the Blockchain quicker. It is very important to be aware of this as usually Crypto which is Stacked is tied up for a period of time (sometimes until an event occurs which itself does not have a specified timeframe).

DeFi has also introduced the concept of a Stablecoin. This has arisen as an attempt to move away from the inherit volatility of Cryptocurrencies by linking (often referred to as 'pegging') the Crypto to an external asset – usually a fiat currency like the US Dollar or gold. In essence, the Crypto is backed by, say, the US Dollar so that the value of Crypto issued is also pegged in US Dollars and held in reserve. As a third party is involved with a Stablecoin, there is a risk that the assets held in reserve may not meet the required value to maintain the stability of the coin, and it also means the party providing the Stablecoin has more control over the Crypto Assets itself, which is not usually the case with Cryptocurrencies.

DeFi products held by the Deceased can create an extra level of complexity for those administering their estate. For example, any Crypto which is Stacked may create big issues around liquidity and for the estate this could lead to difficulties in funding any Inheritance Tax liability. For Personal Representatives, there may also be difficult choices around whether to retain DeFi products which are potentially creating good returns on investment or to encash such assets (if possible) to solidify the estate's position. In a situation where Beneficiaries of an estate may criticise Personal Representatives for a loss of income or growth where Crypto is removed from such Defi products, or similarly for a loss where Crypto remains within such DeFi products, it can lead to difficult decisions being made by the Personal Representative. These decisions will be even more difficult if the Personal Representatives, or those Probate Practitioners advising them, are unaware of these types of arrangements and, for the latter, could indeed lead to a negligence claim if appropriate advice is not provided to the Personal Representative.

Due to the often unregulated nature of DiFi products, this area is also open to a lot of abuse in the form of scams. Again, Probate Practitioners need to be aware of the types of Crypto held by the Deceased to ensure that any questionable DeFi products can be identified as quickly as possible and attempts made to recover any investments made. Appropriate advice should be sought from specialists in the Crypto and DeFi investment space.

CHAPTER FIVE

NFTs

Non-Fungible Tokens ("NFTs") are a unique digital representation of an asset held on a Blockchain. Whilst there are many use cases for NFTs, presently their popularity is centred around digital artwork, collectables and rarities. Many NFTs only exist in digital form – such as crypto-pets, crypto-artwork and such, however, they can also be digital representations of physical assets, tokenised and stored on a Blockchain, such as a pair of trainers, a video or even a post from social media.

It is the unique, non-fungible nature of NFTs which arguably gives them their value as they are often one-off pieces or limited in number, and this creates a market where popular NFTs can be bought, sold and traded.

NFT are usually created through an online marketplace which allows NFTs to become part of the Blockchain. This process is called Minting, and analogous to coins being minted, once an NFT is minted it is in circulation in the online marketplace. In essence, when an asset is minted to become an NFT, a token is created on the Blockchain which includes all of the metadata relating to the crypto asset and is often underpinned by a Smart Contract. It is the token which proves proof of ownership, the metadate which enables it to be identified on the Blockchain, and the details in the Smart Contract which dictate what is actually owned.

A Smart Contract is a programmed agreement which has the intention of being legally binding on those who enter into it. It is automated, so that if certain conditions need to be met, or certain tasks performed, once they are completed the programme will automatically implement the end result.

This is a very important feature for NFTs and one of which Probate Practitioners should be mindful. For those creating and minting NFTs, they can include provisions for the payment of Royalties within the Smart Contract. Once their creation is sold as an NFT, any forward sale from the initial purchaser, and beyond, will automatically credit the specified Royalty payment (say 10% of any onward sale price) to the creators Wallet. This is obviously important for anyone acting in the estate of an NFT creator, as future Royalties could arise for some time after the date of death, and any works ready to be minted need to ensure they have the appropriate provisions for Royalties and such written into them. However, it is also important to understand that if you are selling an NFT from a collection within someone's estate, the sale proceeds received may be less that initially stated.

Transaction fees are also payable, usually on the creation of NFTs and on future sales and purchases. These transaction fees are often referred to as "Gas" and will also reduce the net sale proceeds received following the sale of an NFT.

It is worth noting that NFTs, like Cryptocurrencies, are also held in a Wallet which is linked to the online marketplace through which it can then be traded.

Like many of the crypto assets available, much of the promotion and marketing of NFTs is still done through 'traditional' online platforms, such as social media. There have been a number of high-profile cases where popular NFT creators have been the victims of having their social media accounts hacked, whereby the hackers have announced fake promotional offers and directed users to provide their Wallet details or access links which have allowed access to users' Wallets following which the Wallets have been defrauded and valuable NFTs stolen. Whilst Probate Practitioners need to be mindful of such legitimate promotional campaigns which can add value to the estate (in the form of Airdrops), they must also be vigilant and alive to the possibility of scams and threats to the crypto assets of the estate, particularly NFTs.

However, not all promotions and campaigns from NFT creators are online, there is a growing trend of in person events, such as minting parties and promotional events at which opportunities to add value to NFTs are discussed and presented.

This is where a lot of NFT creators are able to build a brand around their NFT collections which in turn allows the owners of the NFT to further monetarise their crypto assets. For example, there are cases where owners of NFTs have been able to rent their NFT to individuals for events, or affiliate their NFT with a brand – whether that be an online brand or an in person brand. NFT creators are also collaborating with existing brands to create further assets and value for NFT holders, for example NFTs being turned into limited edition (and expensive) pieces of jewellery in real life.

Whilst it is important to be aware of such opportunities to ensure that the value of the assets of the estate are maximised, it is also important to appreciate what ownership of the NFT entitles the estate to. This can lead to complex questions over Intellectual Property rights and infringements.

This becomes a complex issue because it operates on different levels. Fundamentally, there is the underlying assets which makes up the NFT. If this has intellectual property rights associated with it (such as copyright) this may not have been owned by the person minting the NFT in the first place so they would never have the authority to assign this to a purchaser. If the creator of the NFT does own all intellectual property rights to it, the next difficulty is in understanding what rights have been included in the purchase of the NFT. For example, many NFTs will only give a purchaser a licence to use, copy and display the NFT. This can have practical implications if the NFT is to be used in physical form, such as printed on merchandise like t-shirts or hats as the owner of the NFT may not have the right to do this. Infringement of intellectual property rights by the deceased during their lifetime can therefore leave the estate open to claims if such infringements were to be pursued by the creator of the NFT or original owner of the underlying asset.

It is also important to understand that NFTs can be plagiarised and faked. Whilst the data on the Blockchain will show that any such copy or fake is not the real, original NFT, this may not be so obvious on an marketplace where NFTs are listed for sale. This can add further issues for Probate Practitioners who may find the popularity of an NFT owned by the deceased to have fallen due to market mistrust or confusions caused by such copies and fakes, or similarly the deceased may have purchased a copy or fake in error or without knowing it, and the asset which is thought to be of value in the estate could turn out to be worth far less (if anything at all).

If orientating oneself to the world of Crypto coins and tokens was a challenge, the added complexities and issues around NFTs is not for the faint hearted. In light of this, and coupled with the ever increasing volatility in the NFT markets, Probate Practitioners need to be very careful in trying to act too quickly in dealing with NFTs held in the estate of the deceased, as there are arguably a number of moving parts which need to be fully considered and understood before arranging for such assets to be sold or transferred to beneficiaries.

CHAPTER SIX

DECENTRALISED AUTONOMOUS ORGANISATIONS (DAOs)

With Blockchain focusing on decentralised transparency, it is unsurprising that from this technology has arisen a new form of organisational structure.

DAOs are centred around a community which operates under a set of rules, written into a smart contract and sent to members through the decentralised ledger of the Blockchain. Generally, DAOs are democratised as they are collectively owned and managed by their members. Decisions of the organisation are therefore made through members voting on a particular issue, and due to this, DAOs usually issue their own form of crypto token which can be exchanged for things of value within the DAO, but also carry the members voting rights. The DAO crypto token is usually issued as part of a crowdfunding type process whereby members buy tokens in the DAO which in turn uses the monies received for the benefit of the members of the DAO through furthering whatever project the DAO is created to promote and advance.

For example, some DAO's generate funding to buy NFTs and in effect each member then owns a share of the NFTs the DAO purchases, proportionate to the number of tokens they hold in the DAO. Some DAO's are also behind the Defi products which have already been discussed, and are set up in this way to make them as decentralised as possible.

DAO's often have web-based sites where members can also get involved in the projects which the DAO is advancing and in turn earn more tokens by contributing to the collective goal of the organisation.

Whilst membership of and ownership in DAOs may not be commonplace in the estate of those most Probate Practitioners will come across, it is important to have an awareness of them. For example, the deceased may have been very active in contributing to the community and may have content which can be posted posthumously and will in turn add to the value of the tokens held in the DAO.

There may also be important proposals which are made in the DAO and need to be voted on, which could greatly impact the views and values of the deceased whilst also affecting the monetary value of the deceased's interest in the DAO. If a Personal Representative holds tokens in a DAO in which the deceased also held tokens, it also raises the question as to whether the fiduciary duties of the Personal Representative extend to exercising their own personal voting rights in the same way as those held by the estate if this would be most advantageous for the beneficiaries of the estate. It is indeed something Probate Practitioners need to be mindful of so as to advise Executors and Administrators accordingly before they take up their appointment or intermeddle in the estate, if this is something which may cause problems for them in the course of the administration of the estate.

Caution must also be taken when dealing with DAOs, however, because their unincorporated structure therefore means that if there are any proceedings issued against them, judgments enforced or penalties raised by a regulatory body, there is the possibility that this would apply to all of their members. Depending on what form any such action would take, this could lead to unlimited liability falling on, or penalties and sanctions being levied against, the estate.

CHAPTER SEVEN

GAMES

Gaming is a huge industry, and in-game purchases on traditional games consoles and mobile apps is a long-established practice. The downside to this, however, is that the money people spend on in-game purchases (to upgrade characters, buy supplies needed within the game and such) is locked into that platform and cannot be realised. It is therefore very much an investment for the sake of pure enjoyment.

Blockchain gaming has, however, taken this concept to a different level. Games build on the Blockchain still enable in-game purchases, but by combining crypto tokens, NFTs and Smart Contracts, they also allow users to earn whilst they are playing. This is referred to as Play to Earn and the premise rewards users with crypto tokens and/or NFTs the more they interact with the game. Through completing missions, defeating enemies or undertaking quests, players can earn crypto assets. This can either be in the form of a crypto token, which is usually native to the game and can be used to fund further in game purchases, or NFTs which can again be used in the game.

However, crypto tokens and NFTs earned within a game can also be traded on crypto markets, meaning that gamers can buy crypto tokens and NFTs from their fellow gamers in return for other cryptocurrencies which can then be used for real world purchases.

Whilst some Play to Earn Blockchain games are free to play (meaning they require no initial investment from players), others are what is known as Pay to Play, whereby you must first buy a character or crypto tokens with which you can then begin to interact with the game and earn as you play.

Some Blockchain games have also made the characters that gamers use (often referred to as Avatars) NFTs, meaning that they can be traded within the game and generate more value for the users, or can be sold for other cryptocurrencies or fiat currency. Other games are enabling gamers to buy virtual plots of land, on which they can build all sorts of things and add value to the virtual land initially purchased. Again, as NFTs these virtual plots of land can be traded and sold, either for in-game crypto tokens, other cryptocurrencies or fiat currencies. Such games are very much based in the Metaverse which is also a fast-growing concept and centred around Web3.

A further development in Blockchain gaming would be the interoperability of games, where one Avatar, weapon or parcel of land from one game or platform, could be transferred to another game or platform. This would further open up the Play to Earn market and add value to existing crypto tokens and NFTs. Whilst not available yet, given the speed at which this technology is advancing it is certainly something worth noting for the future.

For Probate Practitioners, this therefore opens a new can of worms when ascertaining the extent of a deceased person's estate. Whilst traditional games consoles are usually iconic in shape or name and therefore easily identifiable within the deceased's personal items, Blockchain games do not have a separate console but can be used on any device which supports a crypto wallet. Given the potential value in the assets held within the game, it will be even more important for Probate Practitioners to ensure that no stone is left unturned when reviewing devices of the deceased in order to ascertain whether any crypto assets of value are stored therein.

CHAPTER EIGHT

AIRDROPS

Although not a form of Crypto Assets in itself, Crypto Airdrops are a popular way for startups and new projects to interact with those already on the Blockchain.

Crypto Airdrops are, in essence, a marketing technique whereby new projects or startups will send their new crypto token to users for free. This is also done within NFT communities, where holders of NFTs are then given free crypto tokens to promote the crypto economy within the NFT community.

The aim of Airdrops is often to raise awareness of a new cryptocurrency and encourage those already on the Blockchain to interact with it in the hope that it will gain traction in terms of popularity, usage and value.

Whilst some Airdrops will be unconditional, others will require the recipient to do something in order to obtain the crypto tokens, such as follow a particular person or group on social media, post (or share a post) about the token on social media, create an account and sign up to the new project or community or merely use the tokens on a particular platform or wallet.

As this could generate additional value for estates of the deceased (with little to no effort) it is important to be aware of Airdrops. Not all Airdrops are automatically issued to users, and it may be that Probate Practitioners should direct Executors and Administrators to be vigilant on social media, within crypto projects and on websites dedicated to prompting Airdrops to ensure that the estate does not miss out on any potential increase in value.

That being said, Airdrops can also be used as scams and it is therefore more important to be mindful of how this could cause a loss to the estate.

For example, small amounts of cryptocurrencies may be sent to a Wallet through an Airdrop so that scammers can try to trace the Wallet to the end user – either an individual or company – and then use this information to perform phishing style scams or undertake cyber extortion. This is known as Dusting. Similarly, Airdrops can be used to manipulate the value of cryptocurrencies and artificially inflate the price. The scammers will already have large holdings of the cryptocurrency which they will then sell when the price increased and in turn may crash the overall value of the cryptocurrency. This is known as pumping and dumping.

Probate Practitioners need to be aware of these risks to ensure that Executors and Administrators are not open to manipulation, scams or extortion caused by receiving tokens from Airdrops and doing something thereafter that may jeopardise the estate. It is therefore a fine balance for Executors and Administrators to strike, between not missing out on adding value to the crypto estate, whilst at the same time not leaving the estate open to abuse, attack or fraud.

PART THREE

ADMINISTERING CRYPTO ASSETS

CHAPTER NINE

ACCESSING THE ASSETS

The ideal scenario

In an ideal world, when someone dies their Personal Representatives would be left a schedule of Crypto Assets held by the deceased, the devices on which they can be located and the private keys and seed phrases with which to access them.

Whilst this is only part of the process in administering the Crypto Assets, it would make the process a lot smoother.

The reality

The current reality, however, is in stark contrast to this idealised and organised succession planning.

This may be due, in part, to the average age of those holding Crypto Assets being within a range of people who do not largely question their own mortality and due to this (and usually a rather tragically early death) have not given any thought to the succession planning needed in order to pass on their Crypto Assets.

In many situations, Personal Representatives are left with the understanding that the deceased held Crypto Assets, but with very little else to go on by way of the all-important breadcrumbs which they can follow.

In such a situation where a Probate Practitioner is faced with no real information about the Crypto Assets of the estate, there are therefore broadly three stages to go through in order to begin the administration of the Crypto Assets in the estate; locate, identify and access.

Location

Device Discovery

As a starting point, to locate Crypto Assets it will be necessary to undertake an audit of the deceased's devices.

Physically collecting the devices is an integral step, as family members of the deceased are usually the first point of contact, and if they are not familiar with the devices on which Crypto Assets can be stored, important and potentially very valuable hardware may be overlooked or even inadvertently lost or disposed of. Devices may also be used to store Private Keys and Seed Phrases, and therefore on an initial inspection of the deceased's devices nothing should be viewed as irrelevant.

Whilst there are obvious things which should be collected such as laptops/desktop computers, tablets, mobile phones and external hard drives, some hardware Wallets could be mistaken for pen drives or USB sticks on which someone may assume nothing of importance is held. As mentioned, however, even pen drives may hold important information required to access Wallets once located on devices. As cold storage, they can be ideal vessels within which to save access details.

Having the opportunity to inspect the deceased's electronic devices is therefore highly important, as is the need for the Probate Practitioner to be able to identify potentially important and valuable devices. Obviously, if in doubt take more than you may think is relevant, as it is easer to inspect the devices and discard them as irrelevant thereafter than it is to overlook them in the first instance and then realise (potentially too late) that they are in fact needed.

In focusing on the digital estate, it is also important not to overlook the traditional paperwork which may also be within the deceased's personal items. Whilst Private Keys and Seed Phrases may be written down in analogue form rather than being stored on a device, the deceased may have also held paper wallets. When following the trail of breadcrumbs in search of Crypto Assets, no stone should really be left unturned and this also emphasises the importance of having the opportunity to inspect the deceased's personal effects in the first instance.

Identification

Device Audit

Once you have possession of the devices, it is then a case of accessing them and reviewing the information therein. Care should be taken with this, as it is not as simple as switching a device on and looking around. Notwithstanding the fact that most of the devices may be password or pin protected (which in itself will require expert advice and assistance, particularly if the required passwords and pins have not been left by the deceased), it is important to consider from a risk perspective if your professional indemnity insurance would cover you if you did anything to corrupt the content of the devices which in turn could cause a loss to the estate. It is therefore strongly advised to consider instructing an adequately qualified third party to begin the process of auditing the deceased's devices.

In doing this it will be necessary for perhaps three things to be considered: the first will be overcoming any password or pin protection preventing initially accessing the devices; the second will be searching the devices for any Wallets, apps or Defiapps; and the third will be to look for any documents which may have been created to store Private Keys, seed phrases and/or pin codes.

For example, the deceased may have accessed their Wallet via an external hard drive, and the Private Key for that Wallet may have been saved as a Word document on a pen drive. Similarly, the deceased may have held their Crypto Assets on a hardware Wallet, for which the pin code and pass phrase may be saved on an external hard drive or written down traditionally with pen and paper.

In undertaking a device audit, a thorough investigation should be undertaken. It is the Crypto equivalent of sending speculative letters to all high street banks to see if the deceased held bank accounts for which they have not retained any paperwork. Whilst we now have the benefit of missing asset searches for such traditional financial products, this is not yet the case for Crypto Assets and a more methodical search of devices is therefore required.

One thing that may assist, however, is Cloud Storage and Cookies. In particular, if custodial wallets and exchanges are accessed through an app on a device, the login details may automatically save in the Cookies or be backed up in the Cloud Storage which could help to access those wallets quickly. However, it is important to be aware that if such information is at the fingertips of you or loved ones of the deceased with relative ease, it also makes those accounts and wallets vulnerable to thirty party attacks too. Given that most of these types of services are not decentralised, there is also still the possibility of contacting a traditional 'customer service' team to assist with access.

Access

The results of this audit will then present three scenarios, or a mix of all three. You will either have a note of all devices on which Wallets are held with the corresponding Private Keys/seed phrases/pin codes; you will have a note of all devices on which Wallets are held but will not have any (or only some) Private Keys/seed phrases/pin codes; or you will have a note of Private Keys/seed phrases/pin codes but no details of the Wallets on which they are held. For the purposes of moving forward we will ignore the worst-case scenario of neither finding wallets or Private Keys/seed phrases/pin codes.

As mentioned, on the basis that we do not live in an ideal world, it is likely that you will be presented with the second or third scenario. This is where the basic understanding of the technology comes into play in order to help follow further breadcrumbs.

Given that the Blockchain is a public ledger of transactions, if you are aware that the deceased undertook a specific transaction with their Cryptocurrency – such as a gift to a family member or friend – then there will be a note of the Public Key from which the transaction originated which can then be the starting point for a specialist to try to trace the Wallet. Similarly, if there are multiple Wallets for which Private Keys/seed phrases/pin codes are missing, to narrow the search a specialist can be instructed to, in effect, reconstitute the transactional activity of the Public Keys of each Wallet. This will then hopefully identify those Wallets which have been most active most recently. This may also highlight whether any transactions have been made to a Wallet held by the deceased which was previously unknown.

Once Wallets are located, however, without the Private Keys/seed phrases/pin codes Personal Representatives are faced with a difficult decision. There are organisations who will look to gain access to the Wallets – for want of a better expression they will attempt to hack the Wallet. The difficulty in this is that many such organisations charge a fee of between 20% to 25% of the value of the assets on the device, will usually waiver any liability if the device or Wallet becomes corrupted and therefore inaccessible, and may lack any adequate insurance if access is obtained and there is subsequent fraud on the Wallet whilst under their care.

Personal Representatives could be stuck between a rock and a hard place in deciding whether to risk a targeted attack to access a Wallet, or vacuum seal the device and place it in storage until technology advances sufficiently to break the cryptography protecting the Wallet. If a professional is acting as a Personal Representative, care should also be taken from a risk perspective as a targeted attack could render the device or Wallet inaccessible and leave you open to criticism from the beneficiaries if they were not informed and asked to approve the course of action before the event (and arguably asked to obtain independent advice as part of the process).

As part of a device audit, traditional paper should also not be overlooked. As mentioned, the deceased could have held a paper Wallet which may not be obvious from the digital footprint, and indeed may not be obvious within their personal papers if the family or Probate Practitioner do not know what they are looking for.

However, if the Personal Representatives are successful in identifying the devices, locating the Wallets and then ultimately access the Crypto Assets therein, it is then important to decipher the nature of those assets and secure them for the beneficiaries of the estate.

CHAPTER TEN

SECURING THE ASSETS

Once a Wallet is accessed it is then a case of ensuring Personal Representatives fulfil their key duties of securing and collecting in the assets of the estate.

However, given the various ways Crypto Assets can be held in different types of wallets, together with the growing number of Defi products that are available, this may be easier said than done.

Wallet Audit

As a starting point, once a Wallet is accessed it will be necessary to consider the type of Wallet held and whether this is appropriate. For example, is it a hot Wallet or a cold Wallet; is it a custodian or non-custodian Wallet? A consideration of the pros and cons for retaining the Wallet as it is, or moving the Crypto Assets to a new/different type of Wallet, will be required.

As mentioned, a hot Wallet is open to attack given that it is always connected to the internet whenever the device is, so it may be prudent to move this to a cold Wallet. A lot has also been made of Cryptocurrencies which are held on exchanges as holders on an exchange are in a similar position to people who hold money in the bank, except that exchanges do not get the protection of the Government backed guarantee limit which banks receive in the UK. Having said that, however, there are benefits to holding Crypto Assets in a Custodian Wallet, not least is that they take responsibility for the ultimate transaction which is being undertaken (such as distributions to Wallets held by beneficiaries of the estate).

It is also important to be aware that the deceased may have given other people accessed details to the Wallet or Wallets in question, be it for their own personal use or – more likely – in case there were ever any difficulties in accessing the Wallets in the future. With this possible vulnerability to the assets, it is even more prudent to considering moving Crypto Assets of the deceased to a new Wallet.

Reviewing transactional information on the Wallet may also be prudent. Not only could this highlight any other Wallets the deceased held (to or from which personal transfers may have been made), but it could also highlight potential gifts to friends or family.

Crypto audit

Notwithstanding these considerations, it will fundamentally be necessary to understand the nature of the assets held by the Wallet and how they can be dealt with. The deceased may have held a mix of Crypto coins, token and NFTs, all of which could have nuances in the way they can be dealt with. It is therefore advisable to undertake an audit of the assets (and information) held on the Wallet as soon as possible.

Crypto coins

Crypto coins may be more straightforward in that they have a value dictate by an exchange, which on the face of it offers liquidity to the estate and a way for the coins to be fully secured by encashing them to fiat currency. If time is needed to consider what the beneficiaries of the estate wish to do with the coins, then it may appear relatively easy to move them to a more secure Wallet.

However, if the coins have been staked on an exchange, for example, some contracts governing staked Cryptocurrencies do not allow the staked Cryptocurrency to be moved from one Wallet to another. This not only creates illiquidity, but also means that there are limited options available to the Personal Representatives in trying to move these assets to a more secure Wallet. Whilst it is more reassuring that such coins will not be accessible to any third parties due to the nature of the staking contract, it will be important to understand when the term of the contract ends, whether this is based on a time period or a future event. Ensuring the coins can be immediately secured once the staking contract comes to an end is arguably the best and only solution in such circumstances.

Crypto tokens

Crypto tokens, whilst having a value, may also indicate the deceased's involvement on play to earn games, DAOs or merely an investment in a Blockchain project.

Again, it will be a case of following the breadcrumbs and, hopefully, the previously performed device audit will have also highlighted any apps or platforms that the deceased had access to which could then be 'married up' to the assets in the Wallet. For example, Crypto tokens or NFTs held in a Wallet could relate to a DAO or Blockchain project which is accessed through a platform installed as an app on the deceased's device. A device audit will also, hopefully, reveal if the deceased was mining Cryptocurrencies and, if so, a decision would also need to be taken as to whether this was to be continued or not.

NFTs

For NFTs, it would also be necessary to review the smart contract associated with it to ensure a full understanding of the rights acquired by the deceased. Other arrangements regarding NFTs may have also been entered into, for example, the deceased may have given access to the NFT to third parties in exchange for payment – akin to renting out the NFT which can be done for certain projects, brand affiliation and such. Again, reviewing any such agreements to understand the terms and how this impacts on the estate will be important. Similarly it will be necessary to ensure that if any such agreements have been entered into, no rights retained by the deceased have been breached. It is clear from cases which have been reported about NFTs that a specialist in IP rights may have to be consulted if the deceased had made such arrangements in order to monetise their NFTs.

For creators of NFTs, consideration would also have to be given to any projects which were ready to launch or which were in the process of being produced.

Whilst these things may not in themselves prevent an NFT from being transferred to another Wallet for the purposes of securing it, they may raise wider issues around assignment of rights and the receipt of any future payments.

Deadman's switch

One further point to be mindful of is the potential presence of a Deadman's Switch. In essence, this is something created by the deceased during lifetime whereby they are required to verify transactions within their Wallet within a specified time period and failure to do so triggers the Deadman's Switch which can result in the contents of a Wallet being transferred to a predetermined beneficiary.

Fundamentally, there are a number of issues at play with this type of service. Firstly, from a practical perspective, the non-verification of a transaction could be due to physical or mental incapacity of the asset holder as opposed to death, and if this was the case the Crypto Assets in the Wallet could be transferred during lifetime which is probably not what the asset holder would want, especially if they regained capacity (be it physical or mental) after the Deadman's Switch is triggered. Secondly, given that this authority is provided by the deceased to a third-party provider during lifetime, there is a question as to whether this authority continues after death. In England and Wales, aside from gifts made during lifetime or deathbed gifts, for anything to pass after death it must be conveyed through a testamentary disposition, the legalities of which are set out in section 9 of the Wills Act 1837 which states that it must be in writing, signed by the testator in the presence of two witnesses who must then also sign in the presence of the testator and each other.

It would therefore be prudent to consider whether such an arrangement was entered into by the deceased during lifetime and, if so, take steps to disable it so as to ensure the assets held in the Wallet are not automatically transferred – particularly if they are to pass in terms different to those of the Will or if there is Inheritance Tax to pay.

Having considered the suitability of the current Wallet, the nature and vulnerability of the assets held therein and whether or not there is a need to take any action to further secure the Crypto Assets of the deceased, it will then be necessary to consider what to do with the assets on a longer-term basis.

CHAPTER ELEVEN

MAXIMISING THE ASSETS

Whilst securing the Crypto Assets of the estate is an important step for the Personal Representatives, it is only part of their responsibilities. In having secured the assets, it is then important to ensure the value is conveyed to the beneficiaries. With this, the Personal Representatives must be careful to ensure no financial loss is caused to the estate, which can include a potential loss if asset values and incomes are not maximised.

With more traditional assets, this largely looks after itself. Bank accounts, shareholdings and rental properties will largely automatically continue to generate income through interest, dividends and rental payments which will either be allocated to accounts or accrued until Personal Representatives have authority to collect in the income. Bank accounts also have the protection of the Government backed guarantee limited in the UK which helps to protect the underling capital. Whilst shareholdings and property are at the mercy of market volatility, stockbrokers and estate agents can be instructed to assist and advise on the sale of shares and property respectively in the hope that value is maximised as far as possible. For shareholdings in particular, whilst this may not guarantee maximised value, it does give Personal Representatives reassurance and to a degree protection that they have taken prudent advice in the circumstances.

For those Probate Practitioners advising, or acting as, Personal Representatives of business owners, the ongoing difficulties of dealing with the business interest of the deceased will be all too familiar. However, there is familiarity and, to an extent, a framework for dealing with this. Duties and responsibility from ensuring contractual obligations to customers and employees to the formal winding down or sale/transfer of the business are well known. Again, there are also agents and third parties who can assist with this and it will also usually be apparent that the deceased was undertaking a business and how it was operating (even if it was done badly during lifetime).

For Crypto Assets, however, the Personal Representatives could very much find themselves between a rock and a hard place. The inherently volatile nature of the Crypto market – and the speed at which it can change – means that time becomes a factor in not only trying to decipher what the deceased was holding and how they were using it, but also in obtaining the views and agreement of the beneficiaries of the estate.

In considering income streams, this will largely be governed by the agreements entered into during lifetime by the deceased. As mentioned, any Cyrptocurrencies which are staked will be locked up for the duration of the staking agreement so there will be limited options available with how to deal with these assets. Similarly, any agreements as to the use of NFT artwork by third parties may limit what can be done with those underlying assets and the main focus may be to ensure the payments continue to be received by the estate (see below).

Beyond holding Cryptocurrencies and NFT artwork, there are a variety of other ways the deceased may have generated income from Crypto Assets, as well as holding capital value in them.

Mining

Mining Cryptocurrencies is also a way to generate income. This will usually involve hardware which is not only in itself quite valuable but will be connected to a computer which has mining software installed on it. There are now large organisations which mine Cryptocurrencies on an industrial scale, however, individuals can still be involved in the mining of Cryptocurrencies, which can be as part of a pool of other miners. This in effect allows miners to work more effectively in their endeavours and share the rewards based on their contribution to the pool. Mining can also be set up to be automated so that the devises and software run without the need for human interaction. If the deceased was set up for mining then it will be necessary to carefully consider whether this should be continued or disconnected.

From a practical perspective, it will not be advisable to leave devises running if the deceased's property is unoccupied. The risk of leaving the devise unattended and potentially overheating could, for example, invalidate the home insurance. There are also the associated costs for electricity consumption which would need to be considered in the context of how profitable the mining activity is. Even if the deceased was survived by a co-owner of the property who was willing to have the mining activity remain in situ, again consideration would be needed as to the level of electricity used (and how the costs would be apportioned) and the maintenance and upkeep of the device and monitoring of the mining activity.

Whist a beneficiary of the estate may be willing to take this on, consideration would be needed as to whether this was part of their entitlement to the estate (and whether any value could or should be attributed to the deceased's position in the mining pool together with the value of the hardware and software), or done on behalf of the estate. If the latter, it would be important to ensure that the hardware was adequately insured and that the income arising from the mining was correctly attributed to the estate, particularly if the beneficiary also mines Cryptocurrency personally.

If mining activity is to be continued, it will also be necessary to ensure that any subscription fees for membership of the mining pool continue to be paid.

Gaming

Another income stream for those with Crypto Assets is in play to earn games. The assets within the games will be a mix of NFTs and Crypto Tokens specific to the game. Like mining, to generate more income someone will have to play the game but unlike mining this cannot generally be automated.

It is important to consider whether continued involvement in the game can be undertaken by anyone on behalf of the estate. If this is to be as part of a beneficiaries entitlement then it will be important to understand the value in the game – the NFTs will have an open market value (albeit this may not be known until listed on an exchange for sale) as will the Crypto Tokens of the game which can be ascertained by reference to an exchange. Whether there is any value in the deceased's position in the game and how this can enhance the income earning of the beneficiary would also need to be considered and arguably an expert in Crypto gaming would need to be consulted to ascertain this. For example, because the deceased has reached an enhanced level in the game, does this increase the frequency or level of potential future income which would not be achievable by the beneficiary if they started the game from the beginning.

If a beneficiary offered to continue gaming on behalf of the estate then Personal Representatives should be made aware of the risks in doing this, as in-game trades, poor performance and inactivity can all impact the underlying value of the deceased's assets in the game. It would also be important to check the way in which the game is linked to the deceased's Wallet and whether anyone continuing to game could get access to this.

In most cases it may be more prudent to encash the assets of the game, which is usually done by listing NFTs on an exchange for sale, and converting the Crypto Tokens of the game into a more liquid Cryptocurrency which can then be encashed for Fiat currency.

It is worth noting that Crypto gaming is going beyond the traditional style of game and is positioning itself in the Metaverse. In a nutshell, a metaverse is an immersive digital experience and, synonymous with Web3, is seen by many as the way in which the internet will be accessed and experience in the future.

In some Crypto games, therefore, there is not just a linear narrative of moving through levels or completing challenges and quests, there is a world created where possessions and land can be purchased. International brands and celebrities are also entering this space to merge gaming with real world utility. NFTs within games can therefore be anything from avatars (the digital version of a character, player, pet or creature) and weapons or devices used in the game to parcels of land, digital clothing and names.

It is therefore important for Probate Practitioners to understand the value in this array of assets, particularly with regards to land held in a metaverse and whether this has potential value in the future.

DAOs

The crypto tokens held by the deceased in a DAO in themselves will have some value. The more popular the DAO arguably the more valuable the Crypto Token associated with it, and again they are usually traded on an exchange.

An income stream can be generated from membership of a DAO and this is usually though interaction within the DAO. The idea is, fundamentally, the more you contribute to the digital community of the DAO, the more you can earn in the form of the DAO's Crypto Token. Again, however, this cannot generally be automated and ongoing involvement will be required, with the same considerations as mentioned for Crypto gaming.

However, the ongoing performance of the DAO will arguably affect its value and this can be altered through decisions made by the members of the DAO as the associated tokens usually come with voting rights. For example, one DAO was created with external investment which, due to the success of the DAO over time, was worth a lot of money to the investor. It was therefore proposed by the members of the DAO that the investment agreement be 'altered' so that the investor could only recover their initial investment and not their capital growth return.

Whilst voting the deceased's tokens in such a decision may not have a direct effect on the value of the Crypto Tokens, Personal Representatives need to be mindful of any such decisions which may be voted on in the DAO, particularly if this is immediately before the Personal Representatives are considering the sale of the Crypto Tokens of that DAO, the value of which could fluctuate greatly depending on the outcome of the decision.

Again, expert advice should therefore be sought when considering how to deal with and potentially dispose of the deceased's interest in a DAO.

Artwork NFTs

As mentioned, artwork NFTs may have been let by the deceased and the agreement may impact on what can be done with the capital asset. Whilst it may seem obvious to leave the contract in place and continue to collect the income on behalf of the estate, it is worth noting that the utility the NFT provides is usually also let under such agreements. Opportunities through promotions, airdrops and such could therefore be lost, and it would therefore be worthwhile to consider whether the agreement can be brought to an end early.

If the deceased was a creator of NFT artwork, it will also be important to consider how these assets are dealt with. For example, if a project was at a point where it could be launched it will be necessary to consider whether this should be done. Personal Representatives would need to be aware that listing NFTs for sale – known as 'minting' – comes with a cost. It would be important to weigh the cost of minting the collection with the potential return from sales. When minting the NFTs, the terms of the smart contract governing the sale and the interaction with royalties is also usually set out. It would therefore be essential to ensure this was prepared in the most favourable way possible for the estate, and to also ensure that the Wallet address for any future royalties could be altered if this was not being done through a platform or exchange which allows the redirection of future royalty payments.

Personal Representative would be well placed to discuss this with the beneficiaries to ensure they were in agreement with whatever decision is to be made. This in itself then leads to an important question – which beneficiaries would benefit? If there is a Will with no specific legacy of Crypto Assets or royalties then it is straightforward in that everything falls into residue. However, if there is a specific legacy of 'Crypto Assets' or royalties, would artwork not yet listed on an exchange be included in either definition?

Obviously this would very much depend on the wording of the Will, but it is as much a point for those potentially drafting Wills of clients with Crypto Assets as it is for Probate Practitioners advising Personal Representatives. If the Will is silent on the point about artwork which is held on a device and not yet minted, then some would argue that the artwork on the device is due to the beneficiary to whom the device is bequeathed – or into residue if there is no specific gift of the device.

Speculation

The volatility of the Crypto market has been mentioned previously and is well known. There is therefore a real concern for Personal Representatives that holding any Crypto Asset for longer than is necessary could be viewed as speculation and leave them open to criticism from beneficiaries for any loss arising from this.

Obtaining financial advise from an expert in Crypto Assets is therefore a fundamental starting point for Personal Representatives once they have identified and accessed the Wallets of the deceased.

The choice of encashing certain assets may be limited, however, depending on how those assets are held, in particular certain Cryptocurrencies which are staked. This illiquidity can then have difficulties for the estate, especially if there is Inheritance Tax payable. Given H M Revenue and Customs' treatment of Crypto Assets they will not qualify for payment of Inheritance Tax on an instalment option basis and therefore a loan may be required to pay the tax if there is insufficient liquidity in the estate.

Probate Practitioners may wish to make Personal Representatives aware of the financial products available in the Defi space where lending can be leveraged against the value of Crypt Assets as an option to funding Inheritance Tax. However, care should be taken and financial advice sought in relation to this.

CHAPTER TWELVE

RECOVERING THE ASSETS

Fraud on the Wallet

Many Probate Practitioners will be familiar with the issues that arise on death where Personal Representatives or family members of the deceased claim that assets have been misappropriated either in the lifetime of the deceased (usually towards the end of life when their assets are potentially vulnerable) or soon after death.

There is arguably a greater chance of this arising with Crypto Assets given their decentralised and largely unregulated nature. The number of cases involving Wallets being hacked, exchanges being defrauded and individuals being the victims of Crypto Assets scams his increased dramatically over recent years, and estates will not be immune to this.

If a Personal Representative is faced with such an issue, then there are a number of recent cases which give reassurance that the estate could pursue the stolen Crypto Assets.

The most recent case in this area is Osbourne v Persons Unknown and another [2022] EWHC 1021 (Comm) in which the claimants NFT artwork was stolen from their Wallet and traced to the Wallet of the thief. The claimant argued that the NFTs were held on constructive trust by the thief and that they should be served a freezing order to stop the NFTs being transferred on, with an order for the exchange on which the NFTs were held to provide information about the thief. All orders were granted and served out of the jurisdiction

This followed the decision of the Court in the cases of AA v Persons Unknown [2019] EWHC 3556 (Comm) (involving a computer hack in which a ransom was paid in Bitcoin), Ion Science Ltd v Persons Unknown and others (unreported) [2020] (Comm) and Fetch.ai Ltd and another v Persons Unknown Category A and others [2021] EWHC 2254 (Comm) (both cases involving Cryptocurrencies), which provided similar remedies to the claimants in the respective cases.

Probate Practitioners will be aware, however, of the need for specialist advice in acting for Personal Representatives in the recovery of Crypto Assets, as such cases present unique problems for claimants due to the difficulty in defining Crypto Assets. However, these cases do show the Courts willingness to look to offer remedies in such circumstances.

There have also been cases where a Wallet held on an exchange has been accessed and fraudulent activity undertaken due to a security breach on the exchange. Whilst most exchanges are insured (to a limit) this adds a risk of loss for the estate and additional cost in trying to pursue those responsible for it.

Personal Representatives must also be made aware of the general litigation risk involved with such action, particularly in relation to their exposure to costs. It would be worthwhile considering an application to Court for a Beddoe Oder in such circumstances.

Intellectual Property infringement

Personal Representatives must also be mindful that NFTs held by the deceased may themselves attract claims against the estate – for example if they breach Intellectual Property ("IP") rights. This could arise if the NFT uses work which infringes copyright of the original owner or if it infringes a registered trade mark, and a number of cases have been reported regarding these issues.

Similarly, the NFT itself may have a very limited use depending on the terms of the underlying smart contract. The deceased may have therefore used (and the estate may be continuing to use) the NFT in breach of the original IP rights granted on purchase. If Probate Practitioners are acting for the Personal Representatives of a creator of NFTs, then they must also be mindful that IP rights retained by the deceased may be being infringed which raises the question as to how far Personal Representatives would be required to go in reviewing the way in which NFTs sold by the deceased were being used.

Breach of contract, scams and fall in value

Personal Representatives may also become embroiled in wider issues which, although not unique to Crypto Assets, represent different challenges in how to try to pursue and resolve them on behalf of the estate.

For example, if smart contract underpinning the sale of an NFT are breached then the Personal Representatives may be required to pursue the offending party for any loss. Similarly, if a DAO votes to change or renege on the terms of an agreement which effects the deceased then this may also created issues for the Personal representatives (not least due to the decentralised nature of the DAO).

Scams in the Crypto space are also prevalent, given the value of the market. Traditional Ponzi schemes have reinvented themselves in the Crypto space, whilst fake cryptocurrency exchanges, overly inflated pricing of NFTs and Bitcoin investment schemes have all induced people to lose money when making investments in Crypto Assets.

Whilst there are specialist investigatory services who will act for those who have fallen victim to such scams, they will require specific information to pursue their investigation. Whilst some of this may be available to the Personal Representatives (such as the transaction identifier which will show in the Wallet where the cryptocurrency was transferred, for example), some details of the scam itself may have only been known to the deceased which may make it difficult for the Personal Representatives to provide everything needed to result in a successful investigation.

There have also been recent incidences where Cryptocurrencies have just failed, and their value has fallen to just above zero. If this has happened just prior to the death of the asset holder, Personal Representatives may in such circumstances write off the asset in question. However, it is worth noting that in some circumstances the founders of the Cryptocurrency have tried to give some form of return to investors, be it a partial refund of what was originally invested or an alternative coin or token – a 'failed crypto 2.0' if you will. This is not too dissimilar to some of the equity income funds which collapsed some years ago, from which holders are still receiving small returns on their otherwise lost investments. The biggest difference, however, is in such circumstances the Financial Conduct Authority have a framework within which such matters are dealt with, however, this is not the case for Cryptocurrencies and Personal Representative therefore need to be mindful of how they can stay informed about such matters if they find themselves facing a similar difficult position with crypto assets of the estate.

CHAPTER THIRTEEN

VALUING THE ASSETS

One of the key things to understand about administering Crypto Assets in an estate is their value. For our purposes, the consideration around valuing Crypto Assets is therefore from a practical perspective; what is the assets worth at date of death for Inheritance Tax purposes, and at the time of transfer or sale for the purposes of accounting to beneficiaries. This is not, therefore, an exploration of the correct basis for commonly accepted methods of valuation, nor is it a deep dive into what has become known as tokenomics – an understanding of a tokens economics and the factors effecting its use and value.

With that in mind, it is therefore important to understand that the value of Crypto Assets depends on the underlying asset itself.

Cryptocurrencies and tokens

This would appear to be the most straightforward at first glance, given that cryptocurrencies and most tokens are listed on exchanges (for ease of reference they will be collectively referred to as cryptocurrencies for the rest of this chapter).

There are, however, a few points to consider when looking at the value of cryptocurrencies.

Firstly, the crypto market is open 24 hours a day, 7 days a week and values can be tracked to a specific time on a specific day if necessary. Whilst most activity still takes place within traditional trading hours for stocks and shares, unlike stocks and shares, cryptocurrencies do not have a typical opening and closing value. The quarter up valuation principle used for stocks and shares for Inheritance Tax purposes does not therefore naturally fit with cryptocurrencies.

Secondly, a lot of exchanges price in US Dollars, so you will need to then convert this into Pounds Sterling in the same way you would with any asset valued in a different currency.

Thirdly, some cryptocurrencies can only be purchased using a cryptocurrency rather than with a fiat currency. For valuation purposes it will therefore be necessary to take the value of the end currency, multiply it by the currency for which it will be exchanged which can then provide you with a value in fiat currency.

Finally, and arguably more controversially, what if cryptocurrencies are staked and have a locked in period which is still in place at date of death. Some would argue that the cryptocurrency is illiquid due to the terms of the underlying smart contract governing the staking and as such has no value at that time beyond the income it can generate during that period. As you will appreciate, this would have far reaching implications for Inheritance Tax purposes if this approach was accepted and it is yet to be seen how this would be tested if put to HMRC as part on an Inheritance Tax Return.

One of the biggest considerations in valuing cryptocurrencies, however, is their volatility. Markets can move quickly and prices can fluctuate drastically. This therefore means that Personal Representatives need to be alive to the risks posed to the estate by such volatility whilst also managing the expectations of beneficiaries who may see such volatility as an opportunity. It is also worth noting that fall in loss relief which is available to stocks and shares within an estate is not available to cryptocurrencies.

It is also worth noting that these principles can also apply to governance tokens which are often associated with DAOs and provide the holder with voting rights. Again, whilst many of these governance tokens are listed on exchanges and have readily available valuations, the above factors arguably still apply to them.

NFTs

Whether artwork NFTs or NFTs used in gaming, there is no set method for valuing NFTs.

Important factors to consider include rarity of the NFT, utility, tangibility, liquidity and appreciation value.

As with real world pieces of art, a rare NFT from a specific artist, famous creator or with an affiliation with a well-known celebrity will command a higher value on the market. However, not all NFTs are collectables, and NFTs with a particular utility – be it land or an avatar character in a game, or a ticket for an in person event – can also bring big price tags. The latter also has real world tangibility and the value of the NFT ticket prior to the in-person event will arguably carry more immediate value for its utility and tangibility than it would as a long-term collectors' item after the event.

Other factors such a liquidity (in terms of consumer awareness of the NFT), any associated project and the historical value of the NFT when sold by past owners will also impact the market value of the asset.

It is also worth noting that DeFi products have developed so that someone can now have fractional ownership of an NFT. Despite the nature of non-fungible tokens being unique and singular, they can be split which allows people to invest in them at an affordable level. In practical terms, the NFT is locked up in a vault and a limited supply of token are issued to represent part ownership of the asset. This can in itself increase the value of the asset as the limited opportunity to part own a high value NFT can be very appealing and this in turn can also bring liquidity to the NFT market as the smaller holdings of the NFT can be more readily bought, sold and traded.

This, however, does not make the process for Personal Representative easy when coming to value the fractional share of the NFT. With this, and NFTs generally, it is therefore important to obtain advice around valuing these assets, particularly for Inheritance Tax purposes where it is less likely that the asset would be listed for sale with a price at that time.

Given that a secondary market is emerging for NFTs to be rented out, it would also be necessary to consider whether the existence of any such agreement at the date of death would affect the value for Inheritance Tax purposes. For example, the potential yield the rental agreement could realise may increase the value of the NFT, whilst the term of the rental agreement and whether this can be brought to an end sooner or assigned to a beneficiary may reduce the value of the NFT if it means it is not transferable on death.

One key thing for anyone acting as, or on behalf of, the Personal Representatives of an NFT creator will be the value of any un-minted works. Valuing such works would depend, amongst other things, on a number of factors, including the profile of the deceased, the project they were working on and the success of any previous projects or recent collaborations, the number of un-minted works and such. This would be important for Inheritance Tax purposes, but also for Capital Gains Tax purposes when such works are subsequently disposed of by the estate by way of sale or transfer.

This also raises an important point regarding the drafting of gifts of NFTs within a Will as IP rights and royalties associated with any NFTs gifted in the Will will pass to the specific legatee of that legacy. However, unless specifically stated, un-minted NFTs will not be included in such a gift and the devolution of these assets would pass to the beneficiaries who receive the underlying devices on which they are held. It is therefore important for Personal Representatives to make this distinction, if necessary, when considering the distribution of assets from the estate, as well as for Will drafters to be alive to this when taking the Testators instructions and preparing the Will generally.

The hardware

One thing that cannot be overlooked, but can also not be prematurely dealt with, is the hardware held by the deceased.

Most Personal Representatives will be aware of the going rate for second hand laptops, desktops and mobile phones. However, there will also be value in the deceased's external hard drives, hardware wallets and – although perhaps more niche – mining riggs (which can be very expense and hold their value).

As mentioned, it will be necessary for all devices to be carefully audited for all relevant information and wallet locations, however, once this has been done and the assets secured (subject to any steps needed to secure other digital assets of the estate) the devise could be wiped, returned to manufacturers settings and sold in order to realise more value for the estate.

CHAPTER FOURTEEN

TAXATION OF THE ASSETS

A full review of the tax treatment of Crypto Assets would be a work within itself, and in light of this the focus of the taxation of Crypto Assets for estate administration purposes is limited to raising awareness of the issues for Inheritance Tax, Capital Gains Tax and Income Tax purposes.

Inheritance Tax

Given we have established in earlier chapters that Crypto Assets are classed as property in general legal terms, it is no surprise that H M Revenue and Customs have confirmed that the Crypto Assets held in the estate of a deceased person will be subject to Inheritance Tax.

The starting point will therefore be to value the Crypto Assets as at date of death. General observations about the valuation of Crypto Assets have been made in the previous chapter, but are there any issues particular to the all-important 'Probate Valuation'?

The general principle of having a hypothetical buyer and a hypothetical seller on the open market will apply to the Crypto Asset valuation. Unlike established markets like for example property and stocks and shares, the Crypto Assets market is still arguably in its infancy and it will therefore be important to seek expert advice in valuing these assets to ensure the peculiarities mentioned in the previous chapter and other nuances specific to the Crypto Assets to be valued are not missed in the valuation process. This is particularly important given the volatility in the market and how drastic and sudden down turns of, say, Cryptocurrencies will also impact the wider market and potentially set off a downward trend in the value of NFTs, tokens in DAOs and so on. This is, in part, because the vulnerability of Cryptocurrency values often brings in to question the viability of the underlying Blockchain technology which will in turn impact confidence across the market.

Aside from valuing Crypto Assets as at date of death, it is also necessary for Personal Representatives to make 'reasonable enquiries' about gifts made by the deceased in the 7-year period prior to their death. It is at this juncture for the Personal Representatives where the paradox of transparency and anonymity of Blockchain technology will be most prevalent.

Like flicking through chequebook stubs, the distributed ledger technology of Blockchain will allow Personal Representatives to trace the transaction history of a Wallet and see any transfers of Crypto Assets which may be gifts made by the deceased during lifetime. This could be a transfer of Cryptocurrency to another Wallet address not owned by the deceased, or the transfer of an NFT at an undervalue or for no consideration. Whilst the transaction history will be helpful, it will not tell the whole story as the identity of the recipient may not be apparent. Personal Representatives will therefore still have to ask the question of beneficiaries and friends and family of the deceased as to whether they received any gifts in the last 7 years. Whilst disclosure requests can be made to an Exchange for them to provide the identity of an asset holder, it could be argued that the Personal Representatives would not be required to take this step on the basis that it would breach the 'reasonable enquiries' test for investigating lifetime gifts. It could, however, be something that H M Revenue and Customs may consider exploring in the future if substantial gifts are made during lifetime with no one coming forward to claim them and pay the tax on their value.

It is also important to be aware of the possibility that the deceased may have gifted Crypto Assets to someone by placing them in a Wallet that the deceased created for convenience and for which the deceased retained the access details such as the Private Key. In such circumstances it could be argued that this was in fact a Gift with Reservation of Benefit given that the deceased retained control of the Wallet and could have taken back ownership of the Crypto Assets at any time. If anyone were considering making gifts of Crypto Assets in this way it may be prudent to enter into a Declaration of Trust to confirm that whilst the assets may continue to be held by the deceased, they are in fact beneficially held for someone else.

In declaring Crypto Assets for Inheritance Tax purposes, many of you will be aware that there is no separate Schedule for this asset class (yet). Most commentary from H M Revenue and Customs draws parallels between Cryptocurrency and Stocks and Share so Form IHT411 may be a suitable home for them, whilst NFTs can be viewed as collectables and may fall within Form IHT407. Alternatively, all Crypto Assets could be classed as 'other assets' in Form IHT400 itself with an explanation and breakdown in the 'Additional Information' section of the form. Informal discussions with H M Revenue and Customs seem to indicate that there is no preference as to where such assets are declared, so long as they are in fact declared.

As mentioned above, it is also important to note that there is no relief available for Inheritance Tax purposes if Crypto Assets are sold within 12 months of the date of death at a loss.

One important peculiarity of Crypto Assets is the fact that, aside from holdings on an Exchange or some other forms of safe custody, a Grant of Probate may not be needed in order to encash these assets. This may therefore make it easier for Personal Representative to arrange for any Inheritance Tax liability to be paid within the 6-month deadline. However, it will be important for Personal Representatives to be mindful of the volatility in the market, as considerable losses could arise and be crystalised if Crypto Assets are sold to meet the tax liability. Similarly, substantial gains could be realised, potentially giving rise to a Capital Gains Tax liability for the estate. All options available for funding any Inheritance Tax liability should therefore still be considered by the Personal Representative rather than perhaps using the assets which are the easiest to encash and most readily available.

Capital Gains Tax

A sale or transfer of Cryptocurrencies is a disposal for Capital Gains Tax purposes, unless it is to move such assets from one Wallet to another owned by the Personal Representatives for the purposes of administering the estate.

The same principles will therefore apply on the disposal of Cryptocurrencies by the Personal Representatives as they do on the disposal of any other capital assets of the estate. The ascertained value for Inheritance Tax purposes will therefore be the base cost for Capital Gains Tax purposes, and any market fluctuations between the date of death and date of disposal will govern whether there is a taxable gain to declare. It would seem that any transaction fee and costs associate with exchange rates between fiat currencies if necessary would be a deductible expense for Capital Gains Tax purposes. Similarly, any additional Cryptocurrency acquired during the estate administration period, for example, by way of airdrop, should also add to the base cost for Capital Gains Tax purposes at their open market value.

However, H M Revenue and Customs do not expressly refer to NFTs within their guidance. Instead they merely refer to generic utility tokens which some would argue artwork NFTs are not. Whilst there may be some clarity required in this area in relation to guidance, it would seem logical for NFTs to be subject to Capital Gains Tax like Cryptocurrencies. Due to the lack of guidance it is not clear whether deductible costs of sale would include royalties payable under a smart contract on the disposal of an NFT, as well as the cost of listing it on an Exchange and the associated transaction fee (although the latter points are more akin to Estate Agency fees in the sale of a property and brokerage fees in the sale of shares respectively which are deductible costs for Capital Gains Tax purposes).

It would therefore be prudent for Probate Practitioners to seek expert tax advice in these matters as they arise and make worst case scenario contingencies when considering the Capital Gains Tax treatment on the sale or transfer of Crypto Assets, particularly NFTs.

One final point to note for Capital Gains Tax purposes is the Personal Representatives' statutory powers of appropriation under Section 41 of the Administration of Estates Act 1925. This section of the Act provides that Personal Representatives can appropriate "any part of the real or personal estate, including things in action, of the deceased in the actual condition or state of investment thereof at the time of appropriation in or towards satisfaction of any legacy bequeathed by the deceased."

As discussed, the general legal view of Crypto Assets is as a form of personal property akin to a chose in action and as such the Personal Representatives' powers of appropriation would extend to Crypto Assets. This should therefore be considered prior to any disposal in order to ensure that any Capital Gains Tax allowances which may be available to beneficiaries can be utilised via an appropriation if appropriate in the context of the administration of the estate.

Income tax

In considering the estate administration period, Personal Representatives need to be mindful of the way in which income arising from Crypto Assets should be dealt with for Income Tax purposes.

Any income arising from staking or mining will be treated as miscellaneous income and be taxed accordingly in the hands of the Personal Representatives. This is, of course, on the assumption that the estate will not be classed as trading in these areas. The later disposal of Cryptocurrencies received from these activities will then be subject to Capital Gains Tax as set out above.

If the estate benefits from an airdrop, this will not be taxable income so long as the estate has not had to do anything in return for the Crypto Asset or received it as part of trade.

The Income Tax treatment of income received from Crypto Assets up to the date of death may be more problematic, as it may not be as clear whether or not the deceased was trading during lifetime. Things Personal Representatives must look at during lifetime include the deceased's degree of activity, organisation, risk and commerciality which may be difficult to ascertain. Collaboration with the deceased's accountant (if they had one) will be crucial, but if no advice was obtained during lifetime then it would be prudent to obtain specialist tax advice to clarify this point with a view to voluntarily declaring any unpaid tax which is deemed to be due payable up to the date of death.

CHAPTER FIFTEEN

SITUS OF CRYPTO ASSETS

Where Crypto Assets are deemed to be located is fundamental to the Inheritance Tax treatment of those assets within an estate. However, given the complexity that can arise with questions of situs, domicile, residency and nationality within the context of UK Inheritance Tax, particularly in cross-border matters, it seemed appropriate for the question of the situs of Crypto Assets to be dealt with in isolation.

H M Revenue and Customs' guidance states that Crypto Assets will be situs in the jurisdiction of the beneficial owner. If someone lives in England then their Crypto Assets are viewed as being in England.

Some commentators have, however, highlighted the fact that the courts view Crypto Assets as being situs where they can be controlled. On the basis that private keys govern who can control the underlying Crypto Assets, if the assets are held on an Exchange then it is the Exchange and not the individual who hold the keys. The Crypto Assets in question would therefore be situs in the jurisdiction within which the Exchange is registered.

This question has not yet arisen and has not therefore been tested by the courts. Whilst perhaps not an issue for those who die with an English Domicile (as all worldwide assets will be subject to Inheritance Tax) it will have wider repercussions for those who are resident in the UK at date of death but perhaps not Domiciled here for Inheritance Tax purposes.

In such circumstances it would be beneficial for H M Revenue and Customs to argue that the Crypto Assets of the deceased are situs in the UK given that this is the limited jurisdiction over which Inheritance Tax applies. However, it would be interesting to see the outcome if the Crypto Assets were all held on an Exchange (and had been for some time) based, for example, in the USA as it is suggested that the UK courts may view this as being situs in the US if the Exchange is registered in that jurisdiction and that this should not therefore fall under UK Inheritance Tax laws.

Irrespective of the Inheritance Tax treatment, if Crypto Assets are held on an Exchange which is outside of the English jurisdiction, then it could also arise that an English Will may not govern the devolution of those assets. Instead, the laws of the jurisdiction within which the Exchange is registered may instead dictate to whom the Crypto Assets pass. In federal jurisdictions, this could differ from Exchange to Exchange if registered in different states and it will be important for Probate Practitioners to be alive to this. For those involved in drafting Wills, it may also be an important consideration to discuss with the Testator, because if they have long term intentions of holding Crypto Assets on a particular Exchange outside of England and Wales then they may wish to consider entering into a Will limited to the assets of the jurisdiction in which the Exchange is registered so that those assets can be dealt with specifically by that Will.

CHAPTER SIXTEEN

DISTRIBUTING THE ASSETS

So, having; obtained all devices and relevant paperwork; accessed and reviewed the same; located and accessed all Wallets; established the extent of the Crypto Assets of the estate and secured the same; settled all Inheritance Tax; and navigated the volatility of the Crypto markets, it is then necessary to distribute the Crypto Assets of the estate.

The basic principle for distributing estate assets will apply to Crypto assets as they do to any other asset. It will therefore be necessary to correctly identify the relevant beneficiaries, undertake bankruptcy searches and liaise with the beneficiaries as to how they wish to receive their benefit from the estate.

Arguably, one of the more straightforward methods of dealing with the distribution of Crypto Assets will be to encash all assets and hold them in fiat currency where usual payments by way of bank transfer or cheque can be made to the relevant beneficiaries. In doing this, however, Personal Representatives will have to be mindful of a number of points.

The first are arguably general considerations which would apply to other assets of a capital nature within the estate, such as stocks and shares. This therefore relates to market volatility, costs of sale and exchange rates.

As mentioned, if Crypto Assets have increased in value then it would be prudent for Personal Representatives to consider whether an appropriation of the assets to the beneficiaries would be beneficial to help mitigate any Capital Gains Tax liability. If the assets have fallen in value, then it is important to remember that claim for loss relief will not be available for Inheritance Tax purposes and an appropriation may still therefore be the best course of action so that beneficiaries can carry any such losses forward for their own Capital Gains Tax purposes.

An awareness of the different costs associate with sale and encashment of Crypto Assets is also important. Whilst transaction fees may be the only cost for moving Cryptocurrencies into fiat, the sale of an NFT may not only attract transaction fees but could also result in the payment of royalties (even if sold at a loss from the original purchase price). Exchange rates for the various Cryptocurrencies will also be prevalent (particularly if a gaming Crypto Token, for example, can only be encashed into another form of Cryptocurrency before being paid out in fiat) as well as exchange rates in fiat currencies particularly if a certain exchange or broker will only pay out in say US Dollars.

Aside from this, it will also be important to appreciate issues around liquidity and whether or not there is much of a market for the encashment of certain Crypto Assets, particularly NFTs and even utility tokens of DAOs. Liquidity, as mentioned above, may also be an issue if say for example Cryptocurrencies are staked and locked in for a considerable period of time, or if an NFT is let to someone for an outstanding term with no possibility of bring it to an end prior to the contractual provisions in place. It will be important to have an awareness of these issues to ensure the best possible price can be achieved for the estate (as and when a sale can be effected), whilst also managing the expectations of the beneficiaries.

There are then a number of practical considerations specific to Crypto Assets of which Personal Representatives should be mindful.

Going back to our Wallet distinctions discussed earlier, if Crypto Assets of the estate have been moved to a Cold Wallet then it is important to be aware that, in essence, the person in control of the

Wallet will be 'playing banker'. For Cryptocurrencies, for example, to be encashed it will be necessary to send them to an Exchange where this can be done. It is usual for the address of the Exchange Wallet to be pasted or typed out in the relevant withdrawal section of the Cold Wallet, and ensuring this is correct will be essential to the Cryptocurrency reaching the correct destination and will fall squarely on the person in control of the Wallet to ensure it is correct.

If Cryptocurrencies have been retained on an Exchange then this step will not be required and the Exchange will in essence 'play banker' once instructions for withdrawal are provided. As mentioned, however, should the Exchange become insolvent prior to encashment then all value held with them could be lost.

If NFTs are to be sold, then they will need to be listed on a marketplace and it will then be necessary to decide whether to set a price for the NFT or list it for auction. Similar to the sale of real property in an estate, there is no right or wrong way to do this but advice from a specialist who understands the market will be invaluable in ensuring the best deal is achieved for the estate.

Of course, a beneficiary may prefer to receive their entitlement to the estate in specie so that they can retain the Crypto Assets. Again, in considering this it will be important to ensure the correct Public Key relating to the beneficiary's Wallet is obtained and inputted at the time of transfer. Similar to exchanging bank account details over email or telephone, Personal Representatives and Probate Practitioners should be mindful of the possibility of fraudsters providing false Public Key information and may therefore wish to insist on obtaining such information in person or via secure email.

A beneficiary may not have a Wallet of their own and may therefore instead ask to take ownership of the deceased's Wallet, together with the contents therein, in satisfaction of the share of the estate passing to them. Caution should be exercised in this regard by Personal

Representatives, as future royalties from NFTs created and sold by the deceased could be received into the Wallet in the future which could result in the beneficiary in question receiving more than they were entitled to. The deceased may have also provided access details for the Wallet in question to a third party or set up a Deadman's Switch to provide access information to a third party which had not been triggered at the point of distribution. This could therefore result in a future fraud on the Wallet and raises a question as to whether a Personal Representative could be liable for any such loss due to providing the Private Key for the Wallet to a beneficiary. To avoid this concern, it would therefore be advisable to insist the beneficiary create their own Wallet and transfer the assets to them.

However, some would argue that transferring Crypto Assets in specie could be an AML risk, particularly for anyone acting as a professional Executor. Like the transfer of bullion and precious metals, transferring Crypto Assets in specie could allow a beneficiary more opportunity to claim, or continue to claim, means tested state benefits or evade payment of tax. Ethical guidance may therefore be required if this question were to arise to ensure that no compliance obligations were breached in such circumstances.

CHAPTER SEVENTEEN

DONATIO MORTIS CAUSA

One aspect of lifetime giving which may cause issues in relation to Crypto Assets is the Death Bed Gift – Donatio Mortis Causa.

Picture the scene; an individual has enjoyed the freedom that decentralised Crypto Assets bring, and as a decentralisation purist has, for all of their lives, been reluctant to provide anyone with the Private Keys, Pass Phrases, Seed Phrases or Pins. However, confronted with their own mortality and impending death, they decide in their final days or hours to provide this information to their nearest and dearest family member or friend.

Following their death, the question then arises as to what Crypto Assets the deceased had, where they were held and how they can be accessed. At that time, the recipient of the Private Key then informs the Executor and/or beneficiaries of the estate that the deceased in fact gave the Private Key to them prior to death and as such the Crypto Assets in that Wallet do not form part of the estate as they were gifted to the said individual during the lifetime of the deceased.

Now, whilst such disputes can arise with non-Crypto assets, such as the keys to a property or the chip and pin card of a bank account, this is arguably less common as there are still ways to access a property without the keys or to locate a bank account without the card. However, the Private Keys, Pass Phrases, Seed Phrases or Pins are the fundamental things for accessing Crypto Assets. If part of the allure of such assets is their decentralised nature and the added security they bring it would not be uncommon for access information for such assets to be given to family and/or friends as late as possible, perhaps just before the person's death.

For a gift to truly be classed as a Donatio Mortis Causa it must be made in contemplation of impending death and be contingent on the death, and the gift must be given or delivered and be something capable of being given away in that manner. Fundamentally there must also be an intention to give the asset as a gift as opposed to giving it to someone for safe custody.

In the above example, a lot would therefore centre around the deceased's intentions in providing the Private Key to the individual in question prior to death. However, this in itself could present evidential difficulties and it is foreseeable that this could be a very contentious issue going forward where succession planning for Crypto Assets is left to the 'last minute.'

In discussing death bed giving, however, it is important to draw a distinction between this and Deadman's Switches and other automated methods of passing Crypto Assets on death.

For the latter, it is envisaged that a smart contract can be set up so that once a death is notified to (and presumably verified by) those facilitating the smart contract – or if a contingency event such as verifying an email address or undertaking a specific trade is not fulfilled, then the smart contract would automatically distribute the Crypto Assets in line with the wishes of the deceased as set out in the smart contract.

Fundamentally, it is likely that this would not fall within the definition of Donatio Mortis Causa as it is assumed that the Deadman's Switch or smart contract would not be entered into in contemplation of impending death, but merely as the ultimate fate that will befall us all. If not a death bed gift, then for this to be a testamentary disposition it would have to be executed as a form of

Will on the Blockchain. Whilst the UK Government relaxed the requirements of Section 9 of the Wills Act to enable Wills to be executed remotely due to the global Covid-19 pandemic, it is questionable whether the signing and witnessing requirements of Section 9 as they currently stand could be met electronically or virtually in the context of executing a smart contract to automatically distribute Crypto Assets on death.

Even if this could be achieved, it raises practical considerations as to how any Inheritance Tax would be accounted for and paid (whilst payment could be written into the contract and automatically paid to the Revenue it would be based on the Inheritance Tax rules as at the date of the contract's creation and not at the time of death), any changes that could arise in the devolution of the estate by the deceased making a traditional paper Will, and any disputes arising in the administration of the estate leading to a claim under the Inheritance (Provision for Family and Dependants) Act 1975 or claims of undue influence, coercion or lack of mental capacity.

Whilst a Digital/Crypto Will is not beyond the realms of possibility, until such time as this is legislated upon or tested in the courts, it is difficult to see how a smart contract or Deadman's Switch could be reconciled with the law as it currently stands to make it a valid testamentary disposition.

CHAPTER EIGHTEEN

TRUSTS

It is not beyond the realms of possibility that the Will of the deceased may direct that the Crypto Assets of the estate as a pecuniary legacy, or as part of the residuary estate, pass into an express trust set out in the Will. So for the purposes of the discussions to follow in this chapter, we will assume that such a Will leaves the residuary estate under the terms of a Discretionary Trust for numerous beneficiaries and that the residuary estate is made up of various assets including Crypto Assets.

The first question to address is, therefore, can Crypto Assets be held on Trust?

Whilst the previously mentioned Crypto fraud cases like *Robertson V Persons Unknown* from 2019 and *AA v Persons Unknown [2019] EWHC 3556* viewed Crypto Assets as a form of property, this was in the context of remedial action such as freezing orders.

The New Zealand case of Ruscoe & Moore V Cryptopia Limited (in liquidation) [2020] NZHC 728, involving the insolvency of a crypto exchange, held that Crypto Assets are property capable of forming Trust property. Whilst not binding on UK courts, it is reassuring and gives weight to the argument that Crypto Assets are property and can be treated as such in the context of Trusts.

How are Crypto Assets then vested in the Trustees?

It is well established that a lot of Cryptocurrencies can be held in shares or fractions of units (NFTs can also have fractional ownership), and that there is no way to ascertain which specific Cryptocurrency forms the ownership of that share or fraction of the unit. As a technical point, this therefore leads us to question whether there can be certainty of subject matter – being the intended assets – of the Trust, however, so far this does not seem to have been tested by the courts.

Notwithstanding the possible question over certainty of subject matter, some have argued that the requirements of S.51 (1) (c) Law of Property Act 1925 cannot be met by Crypto Assets. S.51 (1) (c) requires the settlement of an asset in Trust to be in writing and signed by the Settlor. Although this highlights the difficulties of physically vesting virtual assets in the Trustees, some have argued that the transaction history showing the transfer of the Crypto Asset to a wallet under the control of the Trustees would satisfy the 'in writing' test whilst the use of a private key could be viewed as a signature.

From a practical perspective, if beneficiaries were in agreement for the Trust to retain the Crypto Assets (see below) of the estate then it would be prudent for a declaration of trust to be entered into to confirm that the Trustees hold the Crypto Assets (or reference the public key of the Wallet for the sake of clarity) as Trustees of the Will Trust. If there is more than one Trustee, it would also be advisable for all Trustees to have the Private Key for the Wallet to ensure that the Trustees have control over the Trust assets if needs be. For belts and braces Probate Practitioners may wish to consider having an Assignment of Beneficial interest executed to further document the transfer of beneficial ownership from the estate to the Trustees.

Prospective Trustees must also take into consideration the powers of investment available to them, both as set out in the Will and under statute. S.3 of the Trustee Act 2000 provides a general power of investment so that Trustees can invest in anything they would do if absolutely entitled to the asset. However, S.4 of the Trustee Act 2000 requires Trustees to have regard to the Standard Investment Criteria, which ensures Trustees consider the suitability of the investment to be made or retainer, and to diversify where appropriate. Whilst important for all investments, it is particularly significant for Crypto Assets.

Depending on the other assets passing into the Trust from the estate, questions could be raised about the suitability of Crypto Assets passing into a Trust. This is particularly prevalent due to the volatile nature of Crypto Assets, however, if they only formed a small share of the overall residuary estate this may be reasonable. Similarly, if all beneficiaries agree to the Crypto Assets being held in the Trust then this would give reassurance to the Trustees. As for the requirements around diversification, some have argued that the onus is for Trustees to merely consider this and there is no compulsion for Trustees to diversify if they do not consider it appropriate in the circumstances. Again, the consent of the beneficiaries to do this would give further reassurance to the Trustees, as would any provisions in the Will stipulating that the Trustees do not need to diversify.

Given the inherently volatile nature of the Crypto market, Trustees should also check the Will to see if there is any limitation of Trustees' liability for loss in value to the Trust Fund (for example, the Will may state that the Trustees will not be liable for any loss to the Trust Fund if they have acted honestly and reasonably). For Professional Trustees, any such protection is often limited and will not be available due to negligence, and they usually have a duty to obtain financial advice. Given how volatile the market is, it is difficult to see how Crypto Assets would qualify as investible assets for Professional Trustees, however, it may be necessary to balance this with any strong views the beneficiaries may have about retaining the assets, and this should of course be considered in the context of the level of cover available to the Professional Trustees through their Professional Indemnity Insurance.

Whilst not of issue for the purposes of exploring the example of the Discretionary Trust above, if the Trustees had to balance the needs of say a life tenant with those of the remainderman this could also cause issues.

The question over Domicile will also relate to any Crypto Assets held on Trust so it will be important for Probate Practitioners to establish whether Trustees will be on or off shore and where the Crypto Assets of the Trust will be accessed.

Whilst there are still some grey areas in relation to Trusts of Crypto Assets, it would appear that Crypto Assets can be held on express trust but that ensuring all duties and responsibilities of the Trustees are met will present unique difficulties and questions for Trustees and their advisers to consider.

CHAPTER NINETEEN

AML AND COMPLIANCE

Anyone dealing with estate administration in the regulated legal sector needs to be mindful of their obligations when dealing with the assets of the estate. This equally applies to Crypto Assets within an estate, which were ranked as medium risk in the 2020 UK National Risk Assessment. This view was taken due to the pseudo-anonymous nature of Crypto Assets, their global reach through online access and the inconsistency between jurisdictions in the application of regulation in the sector.

One reassuring factor is that Crypto Exchanges and custodian wallet services are regulated by the Financial Conduct Authority in the UK. There is therefore a framework for these organisations to follow when creating accounts for users. However, there are a number of Exchanges and custodian wallets which are located outside of England and Wales, so it is important to understand what, if any, their regulatory requirements are and how they are met.

That being said, given the concerns some people have about the centralised nature of Exchanges and custodian services, coupled with the anonymity cold storage can bring, it may seem more likely that the deceased would hold assets outside of an Exchange or custodial service.

It will also be necessary to consider the Crypto Assets held by the deceased, as some of the alternative Cryptocurrencies which are less mainstream have been viewed as a hot bed for Money Laundering Activity. Some have also highlighted the increased concern around peer-to-peer platforms which are usually direct between two parties in relation to trading and acquiring cryptocurrency. There are no regulated provisions which govern this sort of transaction which again adds to the possibility of Money Laundering or Terrorist Financing being undertaken.

Aside from these issues which are arguably unique to Crypto Assets, there is then the usual need for source of funds and source of wealth to be established. It would not be enough, for example, to see that monies came from a bank account to invest in a Crypto Asset. It will be necessary to justify and understand where that money came from. Similarly, looking at the underlying Crypto Assets, it will be important to consider why the particular assets were purchased and why it was decided for them to be held as they are on death.

Fundamentally, although there seems to be a lack of guidance generally as to how AML legislation applied to Crypto Assets, this is not something in itself which will absolve Probate Practitioners of their duties to ensure that AML legislation is complied with in the context of estate administration.

CHAPTER TWENTY

FUTURE OF CRYPTO

There can be no doubt that Blockchain technology has the potential to disrupt and improve almost every sector and industry on the planet. This seems to be evident in the early adoption in Crypto Assets which has without doubt disrupted the financial sector and continues to permeate retail, hospitality and leisure, music, and fashion just to name a few.

At the time of writing, partnerships are announced on an almost daily basis between Cryptocurrencies and layer two Blockchain tokens, and established financial institutions providing day to day payment infrastructure and retail financial offerings.

NFTs are being incorporated into clothing businesses as digital representations of physical goods, introduced as reward schemes for large hot beverage retailers, as a means of ticket sales for global ticket vendors and are revolutionising the way in which music and IP rights can be distributed, held and monetised.

Play to earn games are being developed to meet the gaming needs of their users rather than the initial intention which seemed to focus on financial needs. Interoperability seems to be the key to unleashing the potential in this sub-sector of Crypto-Assets, and achieving this goal appears to be growing closer and closer on a daily basis. The anticipated value to the market which this would bring is considerable.

The Metaverse, in all its varying forms, is gaining traction with big names in the music industry participating in online music festivals, established fashion labels producing wearables for Avatars and, more recently, in person fashion houses creating cloths designed to look pixelated to replicate the clothing available in the Metaverse and depicted on NFTs.

Despite the level of interest in Crypto Assets, it is clear that the varying sub-categories of this asset class are still very much in their early stages and many argue that things such as NFTs and the Metaverse will not be referred to in the same way using technical terminology once they reach mass adoption and become part of mainstream usage.

Instead, the underlying technology will be incorporated into the day-to-day usability and functionality which will come with mass adoption. Given the considerable estimated value in tokenising physical assets across the mass markets, by the time of mass adoption many of the issues and difficulties currently faced and experienced in dealing with such assets as part of an estate administration will, hopefully, be ironed out and solutions will be presented as part of the accepted process of using these assets on a daily basis.

Until then, however, people will continue to die holding assets which present unique and difficult challenges and it will be important for Probate Practitioners to continue to stay abreast of the fast paced developments and complex technical issues which will invariably continue to arise as this asset class develops. Permeating all of this will, invariably, be volatility in the market which will affect price, liquidity and overall confidence in the emerging technology and the Crypto Assets themselves. This in itself will create challenges for those administering these assets as part of the deceased's estate, not only in ensuring the best interests of the beneficiaries are met but in also protecting themselves in undertaking the too often perilous role of Personal Representative.

Many are arguing that Blockchain technology is here to stay and is already heralding in the next phase of the internet and how we will work, buy, sell, save, earn and play on the internet. Th ecosystem to complete this new wave of technology will also disrupt traditional financial infrastructure and markets and is being pioneered by the Crypto Assets we are encountering today. Whilst it is impossible to predict what they will look like in the new Blockchain centric world of tomorrow, dealing with the issues and understanding how the law needs to adapt and change will continue to present unique and interesting challenges.

MORE BOOKS BY LAW BRIEF PUBLISHING

A selection of our other titles available now:-

'A Practical Guide to Parental Alienation in Private and Public Law Children Cases' by Sam King QC & Frankie Shama
'Contested Heritage – Removing Art from Land and Historic Buildings' by Richard Harwood QC, Catherine Dobson, David Sawtell
'The Limits of Separate Legal Personality: When Those Running a Company Can Be Held Personally Liable for Losses Caused to Third Parties Outside of the Company' by Dr Mike Wilkinson
'A Practical Guide to Transgender Law' by Robin Moira White & Nicola Newbegin
'Artificial Intelligence – The Practical Legal Issues (2nd Edition)' by John Buyers
'A Practical Guide to Residential Freehold Conveyancing' by Lorraine Richardson
'A Practical Guide to Pensions on Divorce for Lawyers' by Bryan Scant
'A Practical Guide to Challenging Sham Marriage Allegations in Immigration Law' by Priya Solanki
'A Practical Guide to Legal Rights in Scotland' by Sarah-Jane Macdonald
'A Practical Guide to New Build Conveyancing' by Paul Sams & Rebecca East
'A Practical Guide to Defending Barristers in Disciplinary Cases' by Marc Beaumont
'A Practical Guide to Inherited Wealth on Divorce' by Hayley Trim
'A Practical Guide to Practice Direction 12J and Domestic Abuse in Private Law Children Proceedings' by Rebecca Cross & Malvika Jaganmohan
'A Practical Guide to Confiscation and Restraint' by Narita Bahra QC, John Carl Townsend, David Winch
'A Practical Guide to the Law of Forests in Scotland' by Philip Buchan
'A Practical Guide to Health and Medical Cases in Immigration Law' by Rebecca Chapman & Miranda Butler
'A Practical Guide to Bad Character Evidence for Criminal Practitioners by Aparna Rao
'A Practical Guide to Extradition Law post-Brexit' by Myles Grandison et al

'A Practical Guide to Hoarding and Mental Health for Housing Lawyers' by Rachel Coyle
'A Practical Guide to Psychiatric Claims in Personal Injury – 2nd Edition' by Liam Ryan
'Stephens on Contractual Indemnities' by Richard Stephens
'A Practical Guide to the EU Succession Regulation' by Richard Frimston
'A Practical Guide to Solicitor and Client Costs – 2nd Edition' by Robin Dunne
'Constructive Dismissal – Practice Pointers and Principles' by Benjimin Burgher
'A Practical Guide to Religion and Belief Discrimination Claims in the Workplace' by Kashif Ali
'A Practical Guide to the Law of Medical Treatment Decisions' by Ben Troke
'Fundamental Dishonesty and QOCS in Personal Injury Proceedings: Law and Practice' by Jake Rowley
'A Practical Guide to the Law in Relation to School Exclusions' by Charlotte Hadfield & Alice de Coverley
'A Practical Guide to Divorce for the Silver Separators' by Karin Walker
'The Right to be Forgotten – The Law and Practical Issues' by Melissa Stock
'A Practical Guide to Planning Law and Rights of Way in National Parks, the Broads and AONBs' by James Maurici QC, James Neill et al
'A Practical Guide to Election Law' by Tom Tabori
'A Practical Guide to the Law in Relation to Surrogacy' by Andrew Powell
'A Practical Guide to Claims Arising from Fatal Accidents – 2nd Edition' by James Patience
'A Practical Guide to the Ownership of Employee Inventions – From Entitlement to Compensation' by James Tumbridge & Ashley Roughton
'A Practical Guide to Asbestos Claims' by Jonathan Owen & Gareth McAloon
'A Practical Guide to Stamp Duty Land Tax in England and Northern Ireland' by Suzanne O'Hara
'A Practical Guide to the Law of Farming Partnerships' by Philip Whitcomb
'Covid-19, Homeworking and the Law – The Essential Guide to Employment and GDPR Issues' by Forbes Solicitors
'Covid-19 and Criminal Law – The Essential Guide' by Ramya Nagesh
'Covid-19 and Family Law in England and Wales – The Essential Guide' by Safda Mahmood

'A Practical Guide to the Law of Unlawful Eviction and Harassment – 2nd Edition' by Stephanie Lovegrove
'Covid-19, Brexit and the Law of Commercial Leases – The Essential Guide' by Mark Shelton
'A Practical Guide to Costs in Personal Injury Claims – 2nd Edition' by Matthew Hoe
'A Practical Guide to the General Data Protection Regulation (GDPR) – 2nd Edition' by Keith Markham
'Ellis on Credit Hire – Sixth Edition' by Aidan Ellis & Tim Kevan
'A Practical Guide to Working with Litigants in Person and McKenzie Friends in Family Cases' by Stuart Barlow
'Protecting Unregistered Brands: A Practical Guide to the Law of Passing Off' by Lorna Brazell
'A Practical Guide to Secondary Liability and Joint Enterprise Post-Jogee' by Joanne Cecil & James Mehigan
'A Practical Guide to the Pre-Action RTA Claims Protocol for Personal Injury Lawyers' by Antonia Ford
'A Practical Guide to Neighbour Disputes and the Law' by Alexander Walsh
'A Practical Guide to Forfeiture of Leases' by Mark Shelton
'A Practical Guide to Coercive Control for Legal Practitioners and Victims' by Rachel Horman
'A Practical Guide to Rights Over Airspace and Subsoil' by Daniel Gatty
'Tackling Disclosure in the Criminal Courts – A Practitioner's Guide' by Narita Bahra QC & Don Ramble
'A Practical Guide to the Law of Driverless Cars – Second Edition' by Alex Glassbrook, Emma Northey & Scarlett Milligan
'A Practical Guide to TOLATA Claims' by Greg Williams
'A Practical Guide to Elderly Law – 2nd Edition' by Justin Patten
'A Practical Guide to Responding to Housing Disrepair and Unfitness Claims' by Iain Wightwick
'A Practical Guide to the Construction and Rectification of Wills and Trust Instruments' by Edward Hewitt
'A Practical Guide to the Law of Bullying and Harassment in the Workplace' by Philip Hyland
'How to Be a Freelance Solicitor: A Practical Guide to the SRA-Regulated Freelance Solicitor Model' by Paul Bennett

'A Practical Guide to Prison Injury Claims' by Malcolm Johnson
'A Practical Guide to the Small Claims Track - 2nd Edition' by Dominic Bright
'A Practical Guide to Advising Clients at the Police Station' by Colin Stephen McKeown-Beaumont
'A Practical Guide to Antisocial Behaviour Injunctions' by Iain Wightwick
'Practical Mediation: A Guide for Mediators, Advocates, Advisers, Lawyers, and Students in Civil, Commercial, Business, Property, Workplace, and Employment Cases' by Jonathan Dingle with John Sephton
'The Mini-Pupillage Workbook' by David Boyle
'A Practical Guide to Crofting Law' by Brian Inkster
'A Practical Guide to Spousal Maintenance' by Liz Cowell
'A Practical Guide to the Law of Domain Names and Cybersquatting' by Andrew Clemson
'A Practical Guide to the Law of Gender Pay Gap Reporting' by Harini Iyengar
'A Practical Guide to the Rights of Grandparents in Children Proceedings' by Stuart Barlow
'NHS Whistleblowing and the Law' by Joseph England
'Employment Law and the Gig Economy' by Nigel Mackay & Annie Powell
'A Practical Guide to Noise Induced Hearing Loss (NIHL) Claims' by Andrew Mckie, Ian Skeate, Gareth McAloon
'An Introduction to Beauty Negligence Claims – A Practical Guide for the Personal Injury Practitioner' by Greg Almond
'Intercompany Agreements for Transfer Pricing Compliance' by Paul Sutton
'Zen and the Art of Mediation' by Martin Plowman
'A Practical Guide to the SRA Principles, Individual and Law Firm Codes of Conduct 2019 – What Every Law Firm Needs to Know' by Paul Bennett
'A Practical Guide to Adoption for Family Lawyers' by Graham Pegg
'A Practical Guide to Industrial Disease Claims' by Andrew Mckie & Ian Skeate
'A Practical Guide to Redundancy' by Philip Hyland
'A Practical Guide to Vicarious Liability' by Mariel Irvine
'A Practical Guide to Applications for Landlord's Consent and Variation of Leases' by Mark Shelton
'A Practical Guide to Relief from Sanctions Post-Mitchell and Denton' by Peter Causton

'A Practical Guide to Equity Release for Advisors' by Paul Sams
'A Practical Guide to Financial Services Claims' by Chris Hegarty
'The Law of Houses in Multiple Occupation: A Practical Guide to HMO Proceedings' by Julian Hunt
'Occupiers, Highways and Defective Premises Claims: A Practical Guide Post-Jackson – 2nd Edition' by Andrew Mckie
'A Practical Guide to Financial Ombudsman Service Claims' by Adam Temple & Robert Scrivenor
'A Practical Guide to Advising Schools on Employment Law' by Jonathan Holden
'A Practical Guide to Running Housing Disrepair and Cavity Wall Claims: 2nd Edition' by Andrew Mckie & Ian Skeate
'A Practical Guide to Holiday Sickness Claims – 2nd Edition' by Andrew Mckie & Ian Skeate
'Arguments and Tactics for Personal Injury and Clinical Negligence Claims' by Dorian Williams
'A Practical Guide to Drone Law' by Rufus Ballaster, Andrew Firman, Eleanor Clot
'A Practical Guide to Compliance for Personal Injury Firms Working With Claims Management Companies' by Paul Bennett
'RTA Allegations of Fraud in a Post-Jackson Era: The Handbook – 2nd Edition' by Andrew Mckie
'RTA Personal Injury Claims: A Practical Guide Post-Jackson' by Andrew Mckie
'On Experts: CPR35 for Lawyers and Experts' by David Boyle
'An Introduction to Personal Injury Law' by David Boyle

These books and more are available to order online direct from the publisher at www.lawbriefpublishing.com, where you can also read free sample chapters. For any queries, contact us on 0844 587 2383 or mail@lawbriefpublishing.com.

Our books are also usually in stock at www.amazon.co.uk with free next day delivery for Prime members, and at good legal bookshops such as Wildy & Sons.

We are regularly launching new books in our series of practical day-to-day practitioners' guides. Visit our website and join our free newsletter to be kept informed and to receive special offers, free chapters, etc.

You can also follow us on Twitter at www.twitter.com/lawbriefpub.

www.ingramcontent.com/pod-product-compliance
Ingram Content Group UK Ltd.
Pitfield, Milton Keynes, MK11 3LW, UK
UKHW020149290926
15471UKWH00004B/775

9 781914 608629